I0126119

# The Circular Economy in Granada, Spain

**OECD**

BETTER POLICIES FOR BETTER LIVES

This document, as well as any data and map included herein, are without prejudice to the status of or sovereignty over any territory, to the delimitation of international frontiers and boundaries and to the name of any territory, city or area.

**Please cite this publication as:**
OECD (2021), *The Circular Economy in Granada, Spain*, OECD Urban Studies, OECD Publishing, Paris, *https://doi.org/10.1787/5f8bd827-en*.


ISBN 978-92-64-63935-5 (print)
ISBN 978-92-64-51034-0 (pdf)
ISBN 978-92-64-55459-7 (HTML)
ISBN 978-92-64-83131-5 (epub)


OECD Urban Studies
ISSN 2707-3432 (print)
ISSN 2707-3440 (online)

# Preface

The COVID-19 crisis has raised awareness of the unsustainable nature of certain environmental and social trends and provided renewed momentum for action on production and consumption patterns, in particular by capitalising on the potential of the circular economy. Whilst many firms are already beginning to embrace the benefits of the circular economy, as they move away from "take-make-dispose" linear systems, these efforts need to be supported by policies, governance structures, and legal and regulatory frameworks that are coherent across policy spaces, ensure all stakeholders are engaged, and that can foster innovation.

Because there is a very strong spatial dimension in these enabling mechanisms, and which is also inherent in achieving an effective circular economy, cities and regions have a powerful role to play in driving this transformation.

This report, which reflects the outcome of a two-year inclusive policy dialogue with more than 70 stakeholders, and draws on the benefit, expertise and guidance of peer-cities, analyses the potential of the circular economy in the city of Granada.

The report includes a number of recommendations and concrete actions that the city can undertake to promote, facilitate and enable this transition, capitalising on its political leadership and manifest commitment to develop multi-stakeholder and multi-sectoral approaches that can drive the transition to sustainable pathways, as well as, new business models.

Granada is at the beginning of its transition from a linear to a circular economy but through its commitment to implement these recommendations and to raise their profile within our community and globally, it also has an opportunity to be among leaders, setting a path for other cities to follow.

Through our Programme on the Circular Economy in Cities and Regions, the OECD Centre for Entrepreneurship, SMEs, Regions and Cities (CFE) stands ready to support Granada with this endeavour, which is more relevant now than ever, as we look to recover from the COVID-19 crisis, and make the circular economy part of the solution towards healthier, less resource-wasteful and more environmentally aware societies.

Lamia Kamal-Chaoui

Director, OECD Centre for Entrepreneurship, SMEs, Regions and Cities

Luis Salvador

Mayor, City of Granada

# Foreword

Like many cities around the world, the COVID-19 pandemic has hit the city of Granada hard, with profound impacts on public health, social well-being and the local economy. As of April 2021, the Autonomous Region of Andalusia, where Granada is located, had the third-highest caseload and number of deaths in the country, after Madrid and Catalonia. The unemployment rate in the city of Granada, already among the highest in the country before the sanitary crisis, reached 28.4% in December 2020. In line with other tourism-dependent provinces, the province of Granada saw a significant fall in gross domestic product (GDP) in Spain (12.6% in 2020), the seventh-highest fall among Spain's 50 Provinces.

However, the COVID-19 crisis is also proving to be an opportunity to rethink urban policies towards more sustainable production and consumption patterns. Lockdowns and related measures saw significant reductions in carbon emissions and, in turn, a greater appreciation and awareness of citizens of the benefits that could arise from more sustainable economic and social models. In response, many cities implemented initiatives that built on this momentum, ranging from bike lanes to food banks, and many are now looking to the potential of the circular economy to accelerate that transformation.

The circular economy is based on three principles: i) design out waste and pollution; ii) keep products and materials in use; and iii) regenerate natural systems. By reconfiguring material loops, the circular economy can increase resilience in terms of food and energy security, reliable access to water, sustainable waste management and the future of transport. Cities could regain public spaces and regenerate green areas. More local food production could reduce transport costs, and organic waste could be used to close loops and strengthen links across urban and rural areas. Buildings, made of traceable and recyclable materials, could reduce emissions and absorb carbon dioxide, increase water efficiency and be self-sufficient energy-wise. This will require supportive and enabling regulations, investments, new forms of collaboration and partnerships and a cultural shift towards a more resourceful and less wasteful society.

The OECD Programme on the Circular Economy in Cities and Regions is designed to support the efforts of national and subnational governments in that transition through evidence-based analysis, multi-stakeholder dialogues, tailored recommendations and customised action plans. The Programme relies on a consortium of cities and countries engaged in peer-to-peer dialogues and knowledge sharing activities, including, in addition to Granada (Spain), Glasgow (United Kingdom), Groningen (Netherlands), Tallinn (Estonia), Umeå (Sweden), Valladolid (Spain) and Ireland.

This report summarises the findings from a two-year policy dialogue with the city of Granada, to develop recommendations and a vision for its transition to a circular economy. It draws on existing best practices, catalysed by Granada's own experience with the transformation of a wastewater treatment plant into a biofactory in 2015, which saw the factory go from being an energy consumer to a producer, and contributed to increased water reuse and the production of new material from waste.

These recommendations, along with the set of tools in the OECD's Programme on the Circular Economy in Cities and Regions, such as the Checklist for Action and the OECD Scoreboard on the Governance of the Circular Economy, will support Granada's transition from a linear to a circular economy, and position it as a future reference for the circular economy.

# Acknowledgements

This report was prepared by the OECD Centre for Entrepreneurship, SMEs, Regions and Cities (CFE) led by Lamia Kamal-Chaoui, Director, as part of the Programme of Work and Budget of the Regional Development Policy Committee (RDPC). It is the result of a 2-year policy dialogue with more than 70 stakeholders from public, private, non-profit sectors and representatives from the city of Granada, Spain.

The report and underlying policy dialogue were led by Oriana Romano, Head of the Water Governance and Circular Economy Unit, under the supervision of Aziza Akhmouch, Head of the Cities, Urban Policies and Sustainable Development Division in the CFE. The report was drafted by Oriana Romano and Ander Eizaguirre, Policy Analyst, who also contributed to the co-ordination of the policy dialogue with the local team. Melissa Kerim-Dikeni, Juliette Lassman, Andrea Accorigi and Luis Cecchi, Policy Analysts, contributed to the report.

The OECD Secretariat is grateful for the high level of commitment and support of the Mayor of the City of Granada, Luis Salvador García, as well as to his predecessor in the earlier stages of the policy dialogue, Francisco Cuenca Rodríguez. Warm thanks are also extended to the admirable local team in Granada for the excellent collaboration throughout the dialogue, coordinated by Gonzalo Jimenez Espinosa, Sustainable Development and Research and Development Director (Emasagra), Agustin Castillo-Martinez, General Co-ordinator of Public Works and Urban Development (Granada City Council); and Clemente Vergara Ballester, Sustainable Development Project Manager (Suez Spain). Warm thanks are also due to the local team: Dolores Ayllón Moreno, Sustainable Development and Innovation, Ana María Rodriguez Márquez, Administrative Assistant and Juan Carlos Torres Rojo, General Manager from Emasagra, Federico Sánchez Aguilera, Director of Institutional Relations from Hidralia, as well as Francisco Aranda Morales, General Co-ordinator of Economics, Business and Treasury, Granada City Council, Spain.

The policy dialogue benefited from insights from peer reviewers who are also warmly thanked for sharing their valuable expertise and guidance, namely: Ana Isabel Page Polo, Co-ordinator of Economic Promotion and Employment (City of Valladolid, Spain) and Eveline Jonkhoff, Program Manager Circular Economy (City of Amsterdam, Netherlands).

This report builds on a series of interviews with more than 70 stakeholders (Annex A) during the OECD visit to Granada, Spain (25 - 28 March 2019), a virtual webinar (4 March 2020) and a virtual policy seminar (23 October 2020), as well as insights from the OECD Survey on the Circular Economy in Cities and Regions and desk research. Interim findings and progress results were presented at the 1st OECD Roundtable on the Circular Economy in Cities and Regions (4 July 2019, Paris, France) and the 2nd OECD Roundtable on the Circular Economy in Cities and Regions (31 March 2020, virtual). Stakeholders are also thanked for their written comments.

The report was submitted to Regional Development Policy Committee delegates for approval by written procedure by 3 May 2021 under the cote CFE/RDPC/URB(2021)2. The final version was edited and formatted by Eleonore Morena, and François Iglesias and Pilar Philip prepared the manuscript for publication.

# Table of contents

# FIGURES

# TABLES

# BOXES

**Follow OECD Publications on:**

http://twitter.com/OECD_Pubs

http://www.facebook.com/OECDPublications

http://www.linkedin.com/groups/OECD-Publications-4645871

http://www.youtube.com/oecdilibrary

http://www.oecd.org/oecddirect/

# Abbreviations and acronyms

| | |
|---|---|
| **ACEF** | Amsterdam Climate and Energy Fund |
| **AMA** | Amsterdam Metropolitan Area |
| **$CO_2$** | Carbon dioxydedioxide |
| **Cotec** | *Fundación Cotec para la Innovación*, Cotec Foundation for Innovation |
| **COVID-19** | Coronavirus Disease 2019 |
| **CSA** | *Cluster de la Construcción Sostenible de Andalucía*, Sustainable Construction Cluster of Andalusia |
| **CSIC** | *Consejo Superior de Investigaciones Científicas*, Spanish National Research Council |
| **DaSCI Institute** | *Instituto Andaluz Interuniversitario en Ciencia de Datos e Inteligencia Computacional*, Andalusian Research Institute in Data Science and Computational Intelligence |
| **DIFTAR** | Differentiated tariffs |
| **EC** | European Commission |
| **EDUSI Granada** | *Estrategia de Desarrollo Urbano Sostenible e Integrado en la Provincia de Granada*, Integrated Sustainable Urban Development Strategy Granada |
| **EEA** | European Environment Agency |
| **EFSI** | European Fund for Strategic Investments |
| **EG 2020** | Strategy Granada 2020. Making the Urban Human |
| **EIB** | European Investment Bank |
| **Emasagra** | *Empresa Municipal de Abastecimiento y Saneamiento de Granada*, Granada Municipal Water Supply and Sanitation Company |
| **EUR** | Euros |
| **Eurostat** | European Statistical Office |
| **FAO** | Food and Agriculture Organization of the United Nations |
| **FEDER** | European Development Fund |
| **FUNCAS** | *Fundación de las Cajas de Ahorros*, Savings Bank Foundation |
| **GBP** | Pound Sterling |
| **GDP** | Gross domestic product |
| **GHG** | Greenhouse gas |
| **GPP** | Green public procurement |
| **GPP4GROWTH** | Project on Green Public Procurement for Resource-efficient Regional Growth |

| | |
|---|---|
| **GRAMAS** | *Red Granadina de Municipios hacia la Sostenibilidad* ,Granada Network of Municipalities towards Sustainability |
| **ICC** | Intelligent Cities Challenge |
| **ICT** | Information and communication technology |
| **IEA** | International Energy Agency |
| **INAGRA** | *Ingeniería Ambiental Granadina,* Environmental Engineering of Granada |
| **INE** | *Instituto Nacional de Estadística,* National Statistics Institute |
| **IoT** | Internet of Things |
| **ISWA** | International Solid Waste Association |
| **IUC** | International Urban Cooperation |
| **LabIN Granada** | *Laboratorio de Innovación Ciudadana de Granada,* Citizen Innovation Laboratory of Granada |
| **LFA** | Life cycle analysis |
| **LWARB** | London Waste and Recycling Board |
| **MaaS** | Mobility as a Service |
| **MAPA** | *Ministerio de Agricultura, Pesca y Alimentación,* Ministry of Agriculture, Fisheries and Food |
| **NA** | Not available |
| **OECD** | Organisation for Economic Co-operation and Development |
| **OVAM** | Public Waste Agency of Flanders, Belgium |
| **PIRec 2030** | *Plan Integral de Residuos de Andalucía. Hacia una Economía Circular en el Horizonte 2030,* Integrated Waste Plan of Andalusia. Towards a Circular Economy at the Horizon 2030 |
| **PMD** | Personal mobility devices |
| **PTS Granada** | *Parque Tecnológico de la Salud,* Granada Health Technology Park |
| **R&D** | Research and development |
| **SDGs** | United Nations Sustainable Development Goals |
| **SMEs** | Small- and medium-sized enterprises |
| **SPW** | *Service Public de Wallonie,* Walloon Public Service |
| **SUDS** | Sustainable urban drainage systems |
| **TOTEM** | Tool to Optimise the Total Environmental Impact of Materials |
| **UCA** | University of Córdoba |
| **UCA-UCE** | *Unión de Consumidores de Andalucía,* Andalusian Consumers Union |
| **UGR** | University of Granada |
| **UJA** | University of Jaén |
| **UNEP** | United Nations Environment Programme |
| **UNESCO** | United Nations Educational, Scientific and Cultural Organization |
| **VAT** | Valued added tax |

# Executive summary

While the COVID-19 crisis put many economic activities on hold, notably tourism, a pillar of Granada's economy, and significantly affected people's lives and social well-being, it has also given renewed momentum to deliver more sustainable production and consumption patterns in line with carbon neutrality goals. At the same time, COVID-19 has provided an opportunity to rethink and reshape urban policies, and increased awareness of the circular economy's role in achieving carbon neutrality goals, whilst also stimulating economic growth, creating jobs, and improving people's lives and social well-being. The Spanish Recovery, Transformation and Resilience Plan (España Puede) set aside 37% of funds for its green agenda, including three main policy levers: urban and rural agenda and the fight against depopulation; resilient infrastructures and ecosystems; and, just and inclusive energy transition.

Granada is taking steps towards the circular and low-carbon economy transition. The recent transformation of a wastewater treatment plant into a bio factory resulted in increasing reuse of water and its transformation into energy, zero waste, zero energy and zero $CO_2$ emissions in 2020. The city is now exploring ways to apply circular economy principles in its urban policies, to cover a much broader range of activities, including:

- Services preventing waste generation, making efficient use of natural resources as primary materials, optimising their reuse and allowing synergies across sectors.
- Economic activities taking place in cities to be planned and executed in a way to close, slow and narrow loops across value chains to increase the durability of goods, reduce waste generation and promote sustainable production and consumption patterns.
- Infrastructure designed, built and operated to avoid linear locks-in, to increase resource efficiency, reusing and repurposing.

Granada has the potential to create a circular economy that capitalises on its main strengths: tourism and science. The city could generate positive environmental, social and economic impacts through greater circularity in sectors related to tourism by for example closing loops across value chains in relation to food, housing and mobility. As a city of science, Granada could also exploit opportunities to develop concrete links between digitalisation and the circular economy, using data and technologies that prevent waste and transform it into new resources.

The innovation that the circular economy can bring about has the potential of producing positive impacts and create new businesses and new job opportunities, in a city that, despite recent improvements, still has one of the highest levels of unemployment in Spain (28.4%).

Achieving this transition will however require overcoming a number of challenges, including: policy silos across municipal departments in charge of spatial planning, climate change and digital transformation in order to achieve common objectives and efficient use of human, technical and financial capacities; lack of effective collaboration on waste, water and transport policies across neighbouring municipalities; insufficient human, technical and financial resources to support businesses; and the need to increase awareness of sustainable consumption amongst citizens.

The city of Granada can play a role as promoter, facilitator and enabler of the circular economy but this requires a collective and coordinated approach across all stakeholders and levels of government.

To <u>promote</u> the circular economy, the municipality could:

- Create a dedicated municipal structure for the circular economy to coordinate actions towards the circular economy transition across municipal departments, building on the experience of the Municipal Office of Innovation, Smart City and Funds for Transformation.
- Define a circular economy strategy, starting with an urban metabolism analysis to map resource flows and consulting stakeholders to identify sector-specific goals, supported by financial and human resources for their achievements.
- Promote a circular economy culture, strengthening and expanding existing educational initiatives, as well as leading by example.

To <u>facilitate</u> collaboration among a wide range of actors to make the circular economy happen on the ground, the municipality could:

- Promote dialogue for cooperation on waste prevention and management; local food production and distribution, tourism and transport within the metropolitan area, in collaboration with the Province and the Region of Andalusia.
- Identify synergies across existing and future initiatives in Granada on climate change, smart cities, and waste management to enhance policy coherence.
- Establish collaborations around the circular economy with relevant players, such as technological centres, universities and the business sector.
- Experiment on circular economy projects at small scale (e.g. neighbourhoods) and facilitate territorial linkages with the surrounding rural areas.

To <u>enable</u> the necessary governance and economic conditions, the municipality could:

- Include circular economy principles into Green Public Procurement, and apply life-cycle analysis approaches.
- Explore funding options to accelerate the transition to the circular economy across businesses and in community based initiatives, including through participation in European calls for circular economy-related initiatives.
- Review and analyse the required skills and capacities for carrying out activities associated with designing, setting, implementing and monitoring the circular economy strategy.
- Support businesses by creating an incubator to promote circular economy projects; organising initiatives for the collaborative development of ideas for implementation in the most relevant sectors of the city; and creating a single window for the circular economy for businesses.
- Explore the innovative solutions that big data, the Internet of Things, machine learning and blockchain tools can provide to the circular economy (e.g. real-time information to make last-mile logistics more efficient).

# 1 Socio-economic and environmental trends in Granada, Spain

This chapter provides an overview of the rationale for the circular economy transition in the city, by looking at the main socio-economic and environmental data, trends and drivers leading to a shift from a linear to a circular economy. The city of Granada is well known for its cultural heritage, which attracts thousands of tourists every year. It is also denominated City of Science and Innovation. As such, tourism and science, especially through digitalisation, can contribute to the economic growth of the city, in accordance with circular economy principles.

## The circular economy in cities and the COVID-19 pandemic: Opportunities for a "new normal"

Spain has been hit particularly hard by the COVID-19 pandemic but the recovery provides opportunities to build back more sustainably. As many other cities around the world, Granada has also been affected by the pandemic. With almost 514 000 registered COVID-19 cases since the start of the pandemic and 9 315 total deaths as of 8 April 2021, the Autonomous Region of Andalusia (hereafter Andalusia) has the third-highest caseload and number of deaths in the country, after Madrid and Catalonia (Ministry of Health, Consumer Affairs and Social Welfare, 2021[1]). Of these 9 315 deaths, the province of Granada accounted for 1 578 (around 17%). However, Andalusia is the seventh region with the lowest death rate per capita in Spain (Figure 1.1). While the crisis put many economic activities on hold, notably tourism – a pillar of Granada's economy – the crisis has also been an opportunity to further reflect on sustainable production and consumption patterns. Environmental and social sustainability is one of the pillars of the Spanish Recovery, Transformation and Resilience Plan (*España Puede*): 37.1% of the funds will be allocated to the green agenda. In particular, funds will aim to accelerate sustainability in cities and rural areas (16%), resilient infrastructure and ecosystems (12.2%) and a just and inclusive energy transition (8.9%) (Government of Spain, 2020[2]).

**Figure 1.1. Andalusia COVID-19 death rate (January 2020 – April 2021), versus Spanish regions (TL2)**

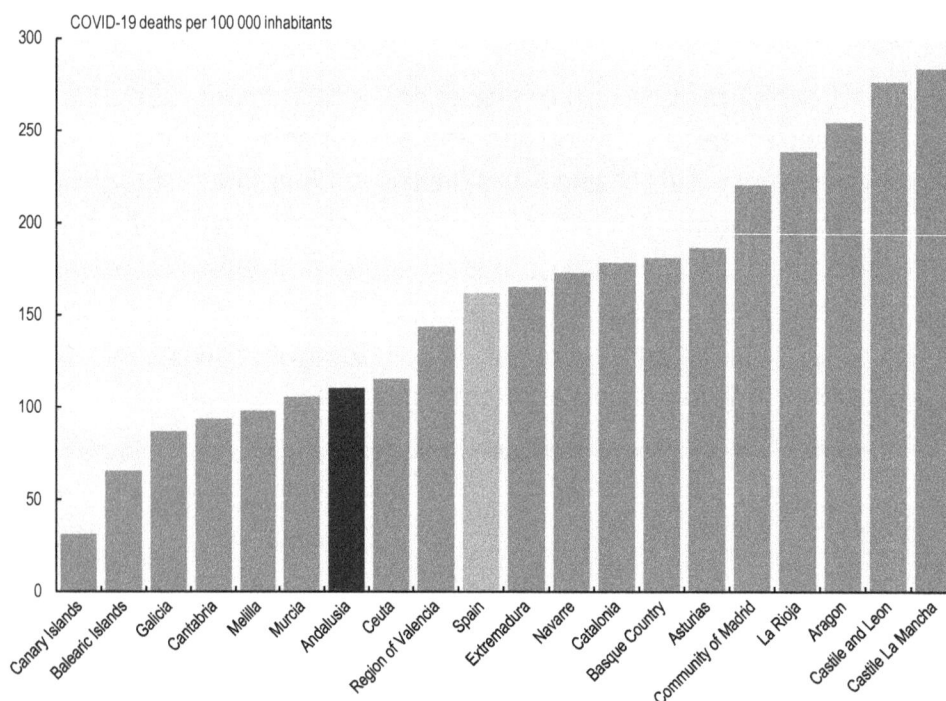

Note: Definition of COVID-19 deaths in Spain: A death due to COVID-19 is defined for surveillance purposes as a death resulting from a clinically compatible illness, in a probable or confirmed COVID-19 case, unless there is a clear alternative cause of death that cannot be related to COVID disease (e.g. trauma). There should be no period of complete recovery from COVID-19 between illness and death. Only in cases of violent deaths or where there is suspicion of criminality or in any other in which a judicial procedure has been initiated is an autopsy carried out (CGCOM, 2021[3]).
Source: Ministry of Health (2021[4]) , Coronavirus Update.

In the post-COVID-19 scenario, the circular economy holds the potential to become the "new normal". The circular economy is based on three principles: i) design out waste and pollution; ii) keep products and materials in use; and iii) regenerate natural systems (Ellen MacArthur Foundation, 2019[5]). According to the OECD (2020[6]), in cities and regions, the circular economy implies a systemic shift, whereby: services (e.g. from water to waste and energy) are provided, making efficient use of natural resources as a primary material and optimising their reuse; economic activities are planned and carried out in a way to close, slow and narrow loops across value chains, and infrastructure is designed and built to avoid linear lock-ins (e.g. district heating, smart grid, etc.) (see Chapter 2; Box 1.1).

---

### Box 1.1. The importance of the circular economy in cities and regions

Being the places where people live and work, consume and dispose, cities and regions play a fundamental role in the transition to the circular economy. By 2050, the global population will reach 9 billion people, 55% of which will be living in cities, high-density places of at least 50 000 inhabitants. The pressure on natural resources will increase, while new infrastructure, services and housing will be needed. Already, cities represent almost two-thirds of global energy demand and release up to 70% of greenhouse gas (GHG) emissions. By 2050, urban dwellers will still be the most exposed to high concentrations of air pollutants. Cities produce 50% of global waste. It is estimated that globally, by 2050, the levels of municipal solid waste will double. A total of 80% of food is consumed in cities. At the same time, water stress and water consumption will increase by 55% by 2050. Moreover, in cities, income inequalities are higher than in other places and rich and poor dwellers live often spatially separated with consequences on equal access to goods and services. The circular economy in cities and regions is expected to reduce negative impacts on the environment in terms of pollution decrease, the share of renewable energy and recyclable resources, the growth and reduction of raw materials, water, land and energy consumption, while potentially increasing resilience and enhancing opportunities for economic growth and jobs.

Cities and regions hold core competencies for most policy areas underlying the circular economy. This includes water, solid waste, the built environment, land use or climate change. In the building sector, for example, cities can operate buildings and housing, and enforce regulation on commercial and residential buildings, in favour of heating, cooling and efficient energy performance. For solid waste, cities exercise powers in collection, treatment, cleaning, as well as in communication and information. Cities have powers over water management, operating infrastructures and incentivising water efficiency, amongst others. Cities and regions can approve land use planning and policies, including zoning, redevelopment and regeneration, encourage farmers' markets and commercial urban food production and develop climate adaptation plans.

According to the results of the OECD Survey on the Circular Economy in Cities and Regions across 51 cities and regions in OECD countries, major drivers for transitioning to a circular economy are environmental (climate change, 73%), institutional (global agendas, 52%) and socio-economic (changing economic conditions, 51%). Additionally, the circular transition is driven by job creation (47%), private sector initiatives (46%), new business models (43%), technical developments (43%) and research and development (R&D) (41%).

Source: OECD/EC (2020[7]), *Cities in the World: A New Perspective on Urbanisation*, https://dx.doi.org/10.1787/d0efcbda-en; EEA (2016[8]), *More from Less - Material Resource Efficiency in Europe*, European Environment Agency; FAO (2020[9]), *Urban Food Agenda*, http://www.fao.org/urban-food-agenda/en/; UNEP (2013[10]), *UNEP-DTIE Sustainable Consumption and Production Branch*, United Nations Environment Programme; OECD (2012[11]), *OECD Environmental Outlook to 2050: The Consequences of Inaction*, https://dx.doi.org/10.1787/9789264122246-en; UNEP/IWSA (2015[12]), *Global Waste Management Outlook*, United Nations Environment Programme; World Bank (2010[13]), , *World Development Report 2010*, http://dx.doi.org/10.1596/978-0-8213-7987-5.

By reconfiguring material loops, the circular economy can increase resilience in terms of food and energy security, reliable access to water, sustainable waste management and the future of transport. Cities could reclaim public space for people while regenerating green areas. Local food production could reduce transport costs, and organic waste could be used to close loops and strengthen links across urban and rural areas. Buildings, made of traceable and recyclable materials, could reduce emissions from material management and absorb carbon dioxide, increase water efficiency and be self-sufficient energy-wise. This will require conducive regulations, investments, new forms of collaboration and partnerships and a cultural shift towards a more resourceful and less wasteful society (Romano, 2020[14]). The COVID-19 crisis highlighted that changes are possible, but that it is important to tackle inequalities (Box 1.2).

---

### Box 1.2. Lessons learnt from the COVID-19 crisis to accelerate the transition towards a circular economy in cities and regions

There are three main lessons learnt from the crisis that can accelerate the transition towards a circular economy:

1. *Changes are possible*: Consumers have changed their consumption patterns. During the first wave of lockdowns in 2020, in all European countries, the proportion of households reporting a decrease in consumption compared to the pre-pandemic period ranged from 18% to 56.9%, and between 3.9% and 30.6% of households reported a total interruption in consumption. On the other hand, many companies showed great flexibility to adapt production to the need for new products or reinvent their business to cope with the decreasing demand and economic crisis. For example, automobile manufacturing companies such as Ford and Tesla transformed their production to manufacture respirators and ventilators, while other companies in the fashion industry (e.g. Gucci and Zara) shifted to supplying surgical masks. Local governments implemented policies that existed before the pandemic but not as politically and socially accepted: from the expansion of bike lanes (e.g. Medellin, Colombia; Rotterdam, the Netherlands; Seoul, Korea) to local food production (e.g. Paris, France) and the creation of city food hubs to avoid food waste (e.g. Milan, Italy).

2. *Act now, but look ahead*: The pandemic required immediate solutions to prevent the spread of the virus, such as the use of facemasks and gloves. While effective from a health point of view, this has led to an increase in the generation of unrecyclable waste. In the United Kingdom, illegal waste disposal has quadrupled. The Irish government announced EUR 1 million in funding to tackle the overwhelming level of illegal dumping attributed to the COVID-19 crisis. In Thailand, the generation of plastic waste increased from 1 500 to 6 300 tonnes per day due to the increase in food deliveries. The global plastic packaging market is forecasted to grow at a rate of 5.5% annually between 2019 and 2021, mainly due to the pandemic. This situation generates a reflection on how long-term impacts should be taken into account when implementing decisions that may have negative effects on human health and the environment, generating future societal costs. In this case, for example, eco-design and reusable products could have helped to reduce the amount of waste produced.

3. *There will be no circular transition without a just transition*: Projections show that transitioning from a linear to a circular economy is estimated to have a USD 4.5 trillion potential for economic growth by 2030. It is estimated that by 2030, the number of additional jobs would exceed 75 000 in Finland, 100 000 in Sweden, 200 000 in the Netherlands, 400 000 in Spain and half a million in France. Whether circular economy policies in cities will be effectively implemented or not largely depends on how green recovery packages will tackle social challenges and inequalities linked to affordability, access to jobs and services (water, waste, energy and transport). The OECD policy paper on cities responses to COVID-19 showed that the crisis exposed inequality across

people and places, especially in large cities, where vulnerable groups such as migrants, the poor, women and the elderly were hit hard. Failing to address these inequalities not only hinders the effectiveness of green policies; it also reduces buy-in and participation in the circular economy transition.

Source: Author's elaboration based on data from: CEPR (2020[15]), *COVID Economics*, https://cepr.org/content/covid-economics-vetted-and-real-time-papers-0; OECD (2020[16]), "Cities policy responses", https://www.oecd.org/coronavirus/policy-responses/cities-policy-responses-fd1053ff/; IFC (2020[17]), *COVID-19's Impact on the Waste Sector*, https://www.ifc.org/wps/wcm/connect/industry_ext_content/ifc_external_corporate_site/infrastructure/resources/covid-19-and-waste-sector; UNEP (2020[18]), *Working with the Environment to Protect People: Covid-19 Response*, https://www.unep.org/resources/working-environment-protect-people-covid-19-response.

# The drivers for the circular transition in Granada, Spain

## *Socio-economic drivers*

Granada is the capital city of the homonymous province and the fourth most populous city in Andalusia. The region is composed of 8 provinces (Almería, Cádiz, Córdoba, Granada, Huelva, Jaén, Málaga and Seville) and is Spain's most populous (8 464 411 inhabitants in 2020) (INE, 2021[19]). In 2020, Granada hosted 233 648 inhabitants, making it the 20th most populous city in Spain (INE, 2021[20]). Its metropolitan area covers 34 municipalities and represented, in 2019, over half of the population of the province of Granada (914 678 inhabitants), which is mainly composed of small municipalities with less than 2 000 inhabitants (Institute of Statistics and Cartography of Andalusia, 2021[21]).

The population of Granada is ageing and shrinking. In 2019, the senior population (over 65 years of age) represented 21.5% of the total population of the city, a figure that is higher than the national (19.4%) and regional (17.1%) level (INE, 2020[22]). Additionally, the population decreased by 4.4% between 2000 and 2020 (Figure 1.2) (INE, 2021[23]). For the 2013-22 period, the National Statistics Institute forecasts a negative population growth of -0.66% for the province of Granada, entailing the loss of 6 085 inhabitants in the census and an average annual loss of 609 Grenadians (Granada City Council, 2015[24]). The ageing trend of the local population can bring changes in energy and consumption emissions. Emissions per capita tend to be lower in households with senior citizens than in households with other age ranges (EEA, 2019[25]).

**Figure 1.2. Population trend in Granada, Spain, 2000-20**

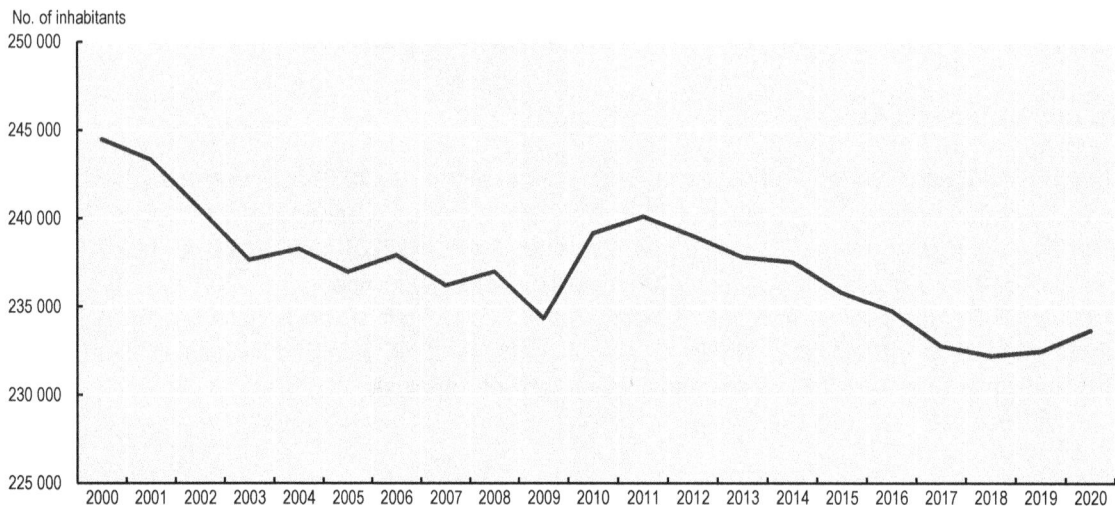

Source: INE (2021[20]), *Población por capitales de provincia y sexo (*Population by Capitals of Province and Gender in Spain), https://www.ine.es/jaxiT3/Tabla.htm?t=2911&L=0 (accessed on 12 January 2021).

Granada attracts thousands of students from all over Europe every year, however the graduate retention rate is low. The University of Granada, one of the oldest universities in Spain and a descendant of the Arab Madrasahs, is the fourth-largest higher education institution in the country. It ranked among the top ten Spanish universities in 2020 (University of Granada, 2020[26]). During the 2019-20 academic year, approximately 55 000 students enrolled in the university, reaching the highest Erasmus exchange rate in Europe (University of Granada, 2020[27]). The number of international students was constantly increasing before the COVID-19 pandemic. The main research areas of the university are artificial intelligence, information and communication technology (ICT), food and health sciences. However, graduate retention rate in Granada is low, as graduates tend to leave the city in search of more attractive work destinations.

Granada is well known for its cultural heritage and one of the most important touristic destination in Spain. Granada hosts the Alhambra Palace, named United Nations Educational, Scientific and Cultural Organization (UNESCO) World Heritage Site in 1984, which is one of the most visited monuments in Europe and the most visited in Spain, with 2.7 million visitors in 2019 (Government of Andalusia, 2020[28]). There are many touristic attractions in Granada and its surrounding areas, including the Sierra Nevada ski resort, the natural areas of La Vega, the Llano de la Perdiz, the Sierra de Huétor. In 2017, with the arrival of 1 786 852 tourists, half of which were international, Granada recorded an average stay of 1.82 days (Government of Andalusia/Granada City Council, 2020[29]). Granada belongs to the UNESCO Creative Cities Network, which promotes cites that prioritise creativity as a driver for sustainable urban development. The city also aims to present its candidacy for the European Capital of Culture in 2031, to be officialised between 2024 and 2025. Granada is seeking to achieve this award by improving and optimising the city's historical heritage, with an investment of over EUR 23 million (UNESCO, 2021[30]; Granada City Council, 2021[31]).

Granada relies on tourism as a pillar of its economy. In 2013, 84.6% of the 22 363 existing firms in the city operated in the service sector, mainly related to tourism, and employed 83% of the total labour force (Granada City Council, 2015[24]). However, certain neighbourhood associations in Granada (especially of the Albaicín neighbourhood) claim that gentrification and unsustainable tourism have resulted in higher rents, despite 85% of stays in 2016 occurring in hotels, with flat rentals (5%) or Airbnb (1%) reported as being less common (Government of Andalusia/Granada City Council, 2020[29]). The city could generate positive environmental, social and economic impacts through greater circularity in sectors related to culture, tourism and hospitality. This would include circular approaches in value chains and policies related to food, housing and mobility, among others.

Granada is a digital hub thanks to its strong specialisation in R&D in technology and artificial intelligence. In 2017, the Spanish Ministry of Economy, Industry and Competitiveness designated Granada as City of Science and Innovation, acknowledging the city as leader for investment in scientific and technological infrastructure. Following this designation, the Municipality of Granada set up the Bureau for Science (*Mesa por la Ciencia*) to promote dialogue and research. In addition to the council, the bureau is composed of the University of Granada, the Science Park, the Granada Health Technology Park (*Parque Tecnológico de la Salud, PTS*), five centres of the Higher Council for Scientific Research, as well as the Granada Confederation of Businesses and the Government of Andalusia (Granada Ciudad de la Ciencia y la Innovación, 2021[32]). Granada hosts the PTS, one of the few technology sites specialised in health in Europe and contributing to the regional strategy for the digital industry, Industry 4.0.; as well as the largest technology and biotechnology cluster in the region, OnGranada (onGranada, 2018[33]). The qualification of the city of Granada as City of Science and Innovation and initiatives for implementing smart solutions in (Box 1.3) could be a way through which to develop concrete links between digitalisation and the circular economy. For example, applications would consist of using data and technology for circular economy models preventing waste, increasing energy efficiency in buildings, monitoring and reducing air pollution through traffic data, transforming waste into resources and regenerating natural systems.

---

### Box 1.3. Digital and smart initiatives in Granada, Spain

There are a number of initiatives in Granada towards a digital transformation and a smart vision for the city, including:

- Granada's Smart City Strategic Plan (*Plan Estratégico Granada Smart City*): Launched in 2018 and in force until 2020, the Plan established the modernisation of the local administration with greater citizen participation, the improvement of private sector competitiveness and the incorporation of ICT in prioritised services related to mobility, the environment and accessibility.
- LabIN Granada: A citizenship innovation laboratory for the brainstorming of ideas, prototyping of solutions and development of projects for the city.
- FIWARE Zone office: To help companies become more competitive by providing advice, training and technical support in the development of "Smart City" solutions.
- Digital Cities Challenge: Together with 15 other European cities, in 2018, Granada was part of the first round of an initiative of the European Commission (EC) that fostered complementarities between existing policies including digital priorities and newly planned actions supporting digital transformation. Polices were the following: Granada Human Smart City, Integrated Sustainable Urban Development Strategy Granada and Granada Smart City Strategic Plan 2020.
- Intelligent Cities Challenge (ICC): Building on the Digital Cities Challenge, Granada joined the EC initiative in 2020. Along with 130 other cities, the initiative aims at developing an innovative ecosystem to drive industrial transformation and intelligent and sustainable growth, while promoting leadership and collaboration among all relevant stakeholders in Granada.

The EC identified three key pillars of Granada's digital community for the design and implementation of a digital ecosystem in the city: i) the University of Granada (especially the School of Computer and Telecommunications Engineering); ii) the Granada Health Technology Park; and iii) the cluster OnGranada, which gathers the main technology-based companies (see Chapter 2). However, some obstacles make the city's digitalisation process challenging. These include the lack of open data, the lack of access to private finance, especially for digital start-ups, and the lack of co-ordination among stakeholders. Nevertheless, digitalisation can enable the circular economy. According to the OECD synthesis report on the circular economy in cities and regions (OECD, 2020[6]) 51% of cities and regions use digital tools to enable the circular economy, while 33% are planning to link digitalisation and their circular economy initiatives in the short term (OECD, 2020[6])

Source: EC (EC, 2019[34]), Assessment Report for the City of Granada: Creativity and Wellness, Core of the Digital Transformation in Granada Digital Cities Challenge, European Commission; OECD (2020[6])The Circular Economy in Cities and Regions: Synthesis Report, https://dx.doi.org/10.1787/10ac6ae4en; Intelligent Cities Challenge (2020[35])Granada, Spain, https://www.intelligentcitieschallenge.eu/cities/granada (accessed on 8 January 2021).

---

Granada's economy is characterised by the service sector. In 2019, the service sector represented 77.6% of the province of Granada's gross domestic product (GDP), slightly higher than the regional (73.9%) and national (74.7%) levels (Ministry of Employment and Social Security, 2020[34]). In contrast, the industrial sector in the province of Granada represented 8.1% of GDP in 2019, below the regional (12.1%) and national (16.2%) averages (Ministry of Employment and Social Security, 2020[34]). In the same year, the agricultural sector represented 7.7% of GDP, more than double the national level (3.1%), while the relative contribution of agricultural employment in the province (8.6% in 2018) was slightly higher than in Andalusia (8.3%) and twice as high as in Spain (4.2%) (Unicaja, 2019[35]). According to the latest available data, in

2015, Andalusia accounted for approximately two-thirds of the integrated agricultural production areas in Spain in 2015, while their distribution varies considerably across provinces and crops (Government of Spain, 2021[36]). In 2019, Granada was the third province of Andalusia in terms of integrated production (70 183 hectares). These areas were dedicated mainly to olive groves (98.4%), as well as almond trees (1.3%) and protected agriculture (0.2%) (Government of Andalusia, 2019[37]).

Unemployment in Granada recorded a downward trend over the last five years but remains high compared to national and OECD standards. Since 2012, the unemployment rate in the city of Granada has dropped from 30.1% in 2012 to 23.2% in 2019, almost aligning with the Andalusian rate (22.3%) but above the national average (14.2%) (OECD, 2021[38])(Figure 1.3). As a consequence of the sanitary crisis, between February and December 2020, the number of job seekers in the city increased by 26.7%, from 22 935 to 29 069, bringing the city of Granada's unemployment rate to 28.4% (Spanish Public Employment Service, 2021[39]).

### Figure 1.3. Unemployment rates in the city of Granada, Andalusia and Spain

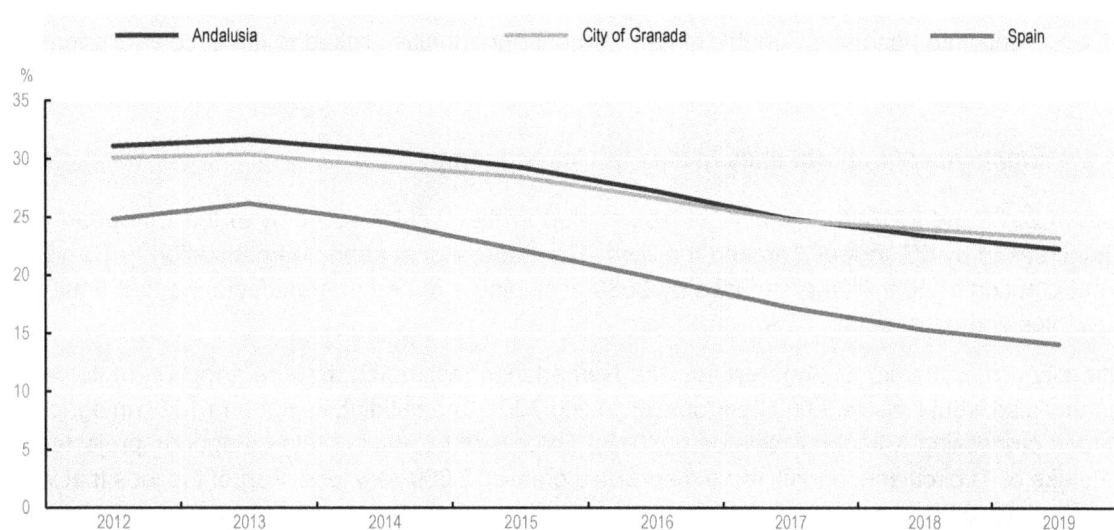

Note: The municipal and regional unemployment rate is calculated as the coefficient between the volume of unoccupied claimants at a given time in a territory and the aggregation of these claimants with the affiliations of residents in this same territory. The national unemployment rate for Spain is measured in numbers of unemployed people as a percentage of the labour force and is seasonally adjusted (OECD, 2021[38]). The unemployed are people of working age who are without work, are available for work and have taken specific steps to find work. The uniform application of this definition results in estimates of unemployment rates that are more internationally comparable than estimates based on national definitions of unemployment.
Source: Own elaboration based on Institute of Statistics and Cartography of Andalusia (2021[40]), *Tasa municipal de desempleo*, http://www.juntadeandalucia.es/institutodeestadisticaycartografia/sima/info.htm?f=j11 (accessed on 19 January 2021) and OECD (2021[38]), , *Unemployment Rate - OECD Data*, https://data.oecd.org/unemp/unemployment-rate.htm (accessed on 9 April 2021).

The labour market in the province of Granada is concentrated geographically in its capital. This is evidenced by the fact that 38.2% of all job seekers at the provincial level in 2019 were affiliated with the social security system of the municipality of Granada (National Public Employment Service, 2020[41]). The average net income in the city of Granada amounted to EUR 21 710 in 2018, close to Andalusian levels (EUR 21 799) for the same year but below the Spanish average (EUR 25 950 (Institute of Statistics and Cartography of Andalusia, 2018[42])).

Potentially, the circular economy can create job opportunities in Granada. In the province of Granada, 9 720 jobs associated with the circular economy were reported in 2018 (Spanish Public Employment Service, 2020[43]). According to the *Prospective Study of Economic Activities Related to the Circular Economy in Spain* report published by the Spanish Public Employment Service in 2020, in 2018, there were 601 894 employees in activities related to the circular economy in Spain, which represented a 0.5% increase compared to 2009 (Spanish Public Employment Service, 2020[44]). Job families associated with the circular economy included the following areas:

- Collection, treatment and disposal of waste; recovery.
- Decontamination activities and other waste management services.
- Rental activities (e.g. cars, leisure and sports equipment, machinery, office equipment).
- Repair and installation of machinery and equipment.
- Repair of computers, personal effects and household goods.
- Retail sale of second-hand goods in shops.
- Sale and repair of motor vehicles and motorbikes.
- Wastewater collection and treatment.
- Water collection, treatment and distribution.
- Wholesale trade of scrap metal and waste products.

Box 1.4 presents international examples of employment opportunities linked to the circular economy.

---

### Box 1.4. Employment opportunities in the circular economy

Between 2012 and 2018, the number of jobs related to the circular economy in the European Union (EU) increased by 5% to reach around 4 million. The International Labour Organization (ILO) projects the net creation of 18 million green jobs by 2030, including 4 million in manufacturing and 9 million in renewables and construction.

At the city scale, the city of **Amsterdam**, the Netherlands, estimated that the adoption of its circular economy plan would create 2 000 new jobs, including 700 in the building sector and 1 200 in agriculture and food processing (Circular Amsterdam, 2016). The city of **London**, United Kingdom, projected that the uptake of its circular economy route map would create 12 000 new jobs. Part of the jobs that will be created relate to the shared economy, as platforms to share resources such as homes, cars, clothing, books and other belongings create new economic opportunities. For example, the mayor of **Chicago**, United States, supported a resource management and exchange platform that worked with Northwestern University and its affiliated hospital system to launch the COVID-19 Emergency Resource Exchange (ERx) aiming to connect frontline workers with surplus masks from tattoo artists, veterinarians and other organisations.

The EC estimates that the implementation of all existing waste legislation will lead to the creation of more than 400 000 jobs in the EU, including 52 000 in Spain. In the country, the transition to a circular economy has the potential to boost job creation in areas directly connected to the environment and nature conservation, including waste management, water and air quality, eco-industries and other sectors. However, these activities have not fully achieved their growth potential; neither have other sectors such as wastewater treatment, environmental R&D, organic farming, forest resource management and biodiversity.

Source: WRAP/Green Alliance (2015[45]), *Employment and the Circular Economy: Job Creation in a More Resource Efficient Britain*, https://circulareconomy.europa.eu/platform/sites/default/files/britain_employment_and_ce.pdf; ILO (2019[46]), *World Employment and Social Outlook – Trends 2019*, International Labour Organization; IISD (2018[47]), "Estimating employment effects of the circular economy", https://www.iisd.org/system/files/publications/employment-effects-circular-economy.pdf?q=sites/default/files/publications/employment-effects-circular-economy.pdf; Circle Economy/Fabric/TNO:Gemeente Amsterdam (2016[48]) Circular Amsterdam - A Vision and Action Agenda for the City and Metropolitan Area, https://amsterdamsmartcity.com/projects/circle-scan-amsterdam .

*Environmental data and trends*

Granada faces important environmental issues but $CO_2$ emissions and air pollution are the main concerns to which the circular economy could provide solutions. $CO_2$ emissions in the city of Granada have remained relatively stable since 2003 but the main drivers of emissions have changed over time. Annual $CO_2$ emissions in Granada have varied between 427 and 502 kilotonnes of $CO_2$, with a spike in 2007 before the global financial crisis and a low point in 2013, but total emissions have decreased by 6.4% overall (Figure 1.4). The importance of road traffic as a driver of $CO_2$ emissions has declined since 2007 but $CO_2$ emissions from electricity generation have been increasing since 2012, both in absolute terms and as a share of total $CO_2$ emitted. The contribution of the domestic sector has remained relatively stable over time, accounting for 19% to 25% of $CO_2$ emissions in Granada.

## Figure 1.4. $CO_2$ emissions in the city of Granada, Spain, 2003-17

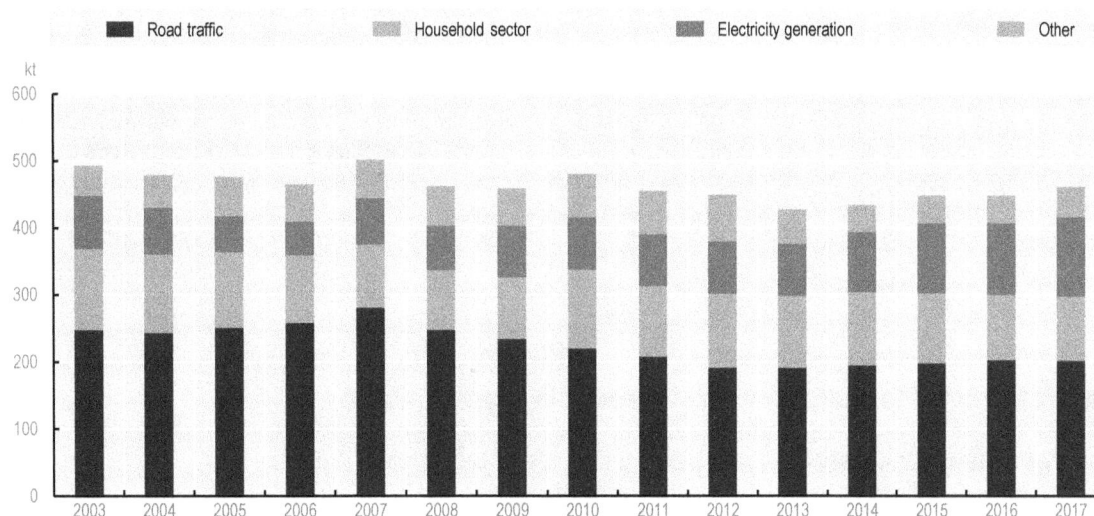

Note: Other includes the following categories: extractive activities and mineral treatment; agriculture; oil and gas distribution; wildfires; waste incineration; food industry; chemical industry; dry cleaning; agriculture machinery; other means of transport and mobile machinery; use of solvents; rail transport; and commercial and institutional sector.
Source: Government of Andalusia (2021[49]), *Inventory of Atmospheric Emissions in Andalusia*.

Granada is one of Spain's most polluted cities, mainly as a result of emissions due to traffic, heating and construction but also due to its orography and climate conditions (Government of Spain, 2019[50]). The city and its metropolitan area are located in a valley surrounded by mountains, a situation that favours the formation of thermal inversions and weak winds, hindering the dispersion of pollution during the winter season. In 2019, the metropolitan area of Granada registered the highest mean population exposure to PM2.5 air pollution[1] in Spain (15.1 µg/m$^3$), above the OECD average (13.9 µg/m$^3$) and the World Health Organization (WHO) standard (10 µg/m$^3$) (OECD, 2021[51]). However, progress has been made over the last decade, as exposure to PM2.5 air pollution has decreased by 22% between 2005 and 2019 (OECD, 2021[51]). Granada has set up initiatives to improve air quality and the transition to the circular economy is believed to contribute to this goal (Box 1.5). Figure 1.5 shows the words that the city of Granada most associates with the circular economy concept according to the OECD Survey (2020[52]). The bigger the word in the figure, the higher the importance. These words are, in the order of priority, "climate change", "environment", "sustainable development", "reusing" and "recover".

**Figure 1.5. Tag cloud on the circular economy in Granada, Spain**

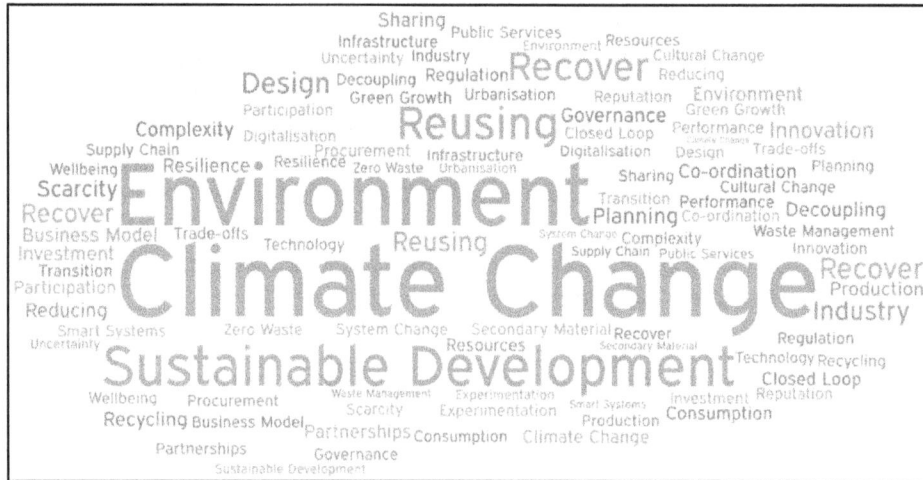

Note: The local team in Granada responding to the OECD Survey on the Circular Economy in Cities and Regions was required to choose the top five words most often associated with the circular economy. The answer is based on the following question: "Please indicate the top 5 words from the list suggested below you most often associate with the circular economy in your context, ranking from 1 (most important) to 5 (less important)".
Source: Own elaboration based on the city of Granada's answers to OECD (2020[52]), *Survey on the Circular Economy in Cities and Regions*, OECD, Paris.

---

**Box 1.5. Measures to address air quality issues in Granada, Spain**

The city of Granada has set up a number of initiatives to tackle air pollution:

- **Planning**: The Municipality of Granada approved in 2017 the first Air Quality Improvement Plan for 2017-20. The plan gathered 36 specific actions divided into 4 horizontal areas (capacity building; information; awareness-raising and collaboration; and management) and 5 sectors (industry; built environment; transport; agriculture and farming; and residential, commercial and institutional). Recognising its promotion of sustainability, notably via the Plan for Granada Towards Sustainability (*Granada caminando hacia la sostenibilidad*) and its efforts to improve environmental quality, the Environmental Forum Foundation awarded Granada the prize of the most sustainable city in Spain in 2019.

- **Introduction of speed limits**: As private mobility is identified as one of the main causes of air pollution, the city limited vehicle speed to 30km/h throughout the city to reduce pollution. Due to the low air quality, citizens have started to demand measures to reduce the amount of traffic in the city. For example, the citizen's platform in the Realejo neighbourhood, "*Por un Realejo habitable*", demands a healthier and safer neighbourhood for citizens.

- **Extension of urban vegetation**: In 2020, the city of Granada signed an agreement with the Plant-for-the-Planet Foundation to develop the Green Ring Road (*Anillo verde*) project for the cultivation of more than 200 000 trees by 2031. The project will start with 2 plots of around 90 000 m² in total.

- **Data collection**: In 2021, Granada started implementing metering systems throughout the city to monitor pollutant emissions in real-time, providing four daily data transmissions. The initiative foresees the installation of more than 300 meters in and around the 2 conurbations that compose the Metropolitan Area of Granada: the Urban Agglomeration of Granada and the

Southwest Metropolitan Urban Area. This initiative for the improvement of air quality complements other measures already in place such as the installation of information panels on municipal buildings and video cameras to raise awareness on air quality.

Source: Granada City Council (2017[53]), *Plan de mejora de la calidad del aire del término municipal de Granada 2017-2020 (Air Quality Improvement Plan for 2017-2020)*, https://www.granada.org/inet/wordenanz.nsf/wwalias/3DA6AC842BD8A240C1258221004B7F52; Provincial Council of Granada (2021[54]), "Diputación comienza en Gójar las mediciones para el diagnóstico de calidad del aire en el área metropolitana de Granada (The Provincial Council begins in Gójar the measurements for the diagnosis of air quality in the metropolitan area of Granada)", https://www.dipgra.es/amplia-actualidad/noticias-inicio/diputacion-comienza-gojar-mediciones-diagnostico-calidad-del-aire-area-metropolitana-granada; Granada City Council (2020[55]), "Nace el 'skyline' verde de la ciudad de Granada, el Anillo Verde (The green "skyline" of the city of Granada)", https://www.granada.org/inet/wprensa.nsf/0284aa18655e179cc1257be5003cc7f9; Granada City Council (2019[56]), "El Ayuntamiento extiende a toda la ciudad la limitación de la velocidad a 30 kilómetros hora (Granada City Council extends 30 km/h speed limit to the whole city)", https://www.granada.org/inet/wprensa.nsf/0284aa18655e179cc1257be5003cc7f9/; Forum Ambiental Foundation (2019[57]), *Premios Ciudad Sostenible (Sustainable City Awards)*.

Regarding the waste sector, one of the pillars of the circular economy, available data at the regional rather than at the local scale, shows that levels of separate waste collection in Andalusia are still relatively low in the region compared to other Spanish autonomous regions and there is no yet ambitious vision for conceiving a paradigm change from waste as a resource. Urban waste per capita collected in Andalusia decreased by 13.4% between 2012 and 2014 but has been growing since then, following the overall trend for Spain (Figure 1.6). In 2018, urban waste collected per capita in Andalusia reached 526.7 kg per capita, over 40 kg above the Spanish average of 485.9 kg per capita, making Andalusia the fourth-highest autonomous region in terms of urban waste collected per capita. On average, 12% of all urban waste collected in Andalusia had been separated between 2010 and 2018, below the Spanish average of 18.6%. The share of separate waste as a share of total urban waste collected in Andalusia remained relatively stable between 2010 and 2018, oscillating between 11.1% and 13.7%, below the overall Spanish level (Figure 1.7). In Spain, separated waste as a share of the total waste collected surpassed the 20% bar in 2018 (20.4%). Responsibility for the different phases of municipal waste separation, collection and treatment is fragmented, and the Municipal Waste Management Programme for the province of Granada 2014-24 does not integrate circularity principles. Data is available at the city level but it is both unclear in terms of the indicators measured and inconsistent with national sources. Integrating circular economy principles into waste management and other economic sectors could help to significantly reduce the amount of waste generated, as well as increase the share of waste separated and recycled (INE, 2019[58]).

Water consumption in Granada is decreasing but wastewater treatment and reuse in Andalusia remain relatively limited. Water consumption in the city of Granada and its 14 adjacent municipalities[2] decreased by 22.6% between 2013 and 2020, from 50 980 350 m$^3$ to 39 439 912 m$^3$, according to Emasagra (2020[59]). In 2018, the average household water consumption in Andalusia was 128 litres per inhabitant per day, just below the national average of 133 litres (EP Data, 2021[60]). Granada has high-quality drinking water, well above the norms established by the WHO, the EU and Spanish sanitary authorities (Emasagra, 2020[61]). However, just 75.3% of the population of the province of Granada benefitted from water treatment (considering plants in operation and still under construction), the lowest rate of all Andalusian provinces and well below the Andalusian average of 89.7% (Government of Andalusia, 2020[62]). Furthermore, just 4.8% of treated wastewater is reused in Andalusia, below the national average of 11.2% (Official Association of Biologists of Andalusia, 2021[63]). Moving from a linear to a circular approach reducing and reusing water can have positive environmental, economic and social impacts, particularly in water-scarce areas such as Andalusia.

### Figure 1.6. Collected municipal waste in Andalusia and Spain, 2010-18

Per capita per year (kg)

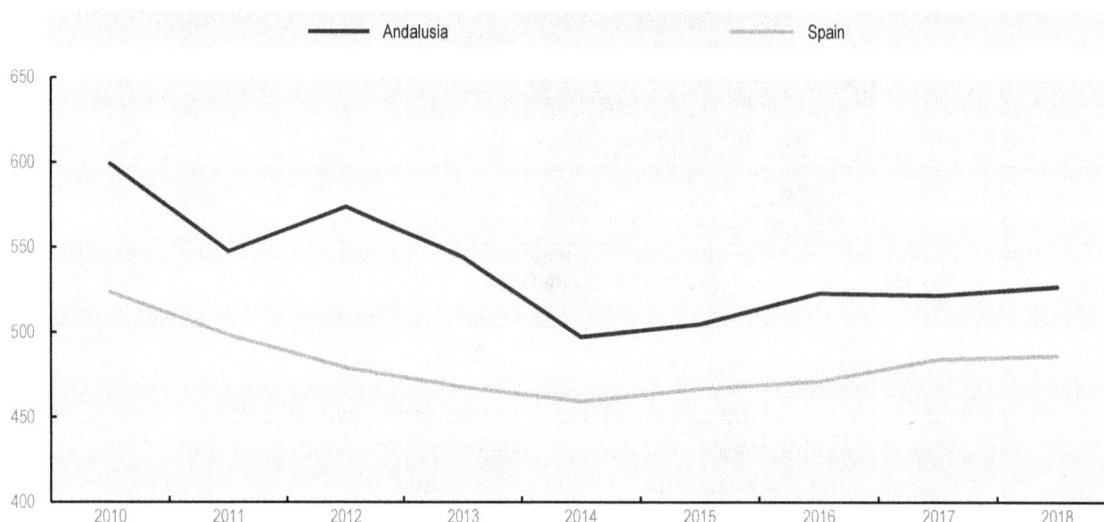

Source: INE (2019[58]), Estadísticas sobre recogida y tratamiento de residuos. Residuos urbanos: Serie 2010-2018, https://www.ine.es/jaxi/T abla.htm?path=/t26/e068/p01/serie/l0/&file=02003.px&L=0.

### Figure 1.7. Separated municipal waste in Andalusia and Spain, 2010-18

Share of total waste collected

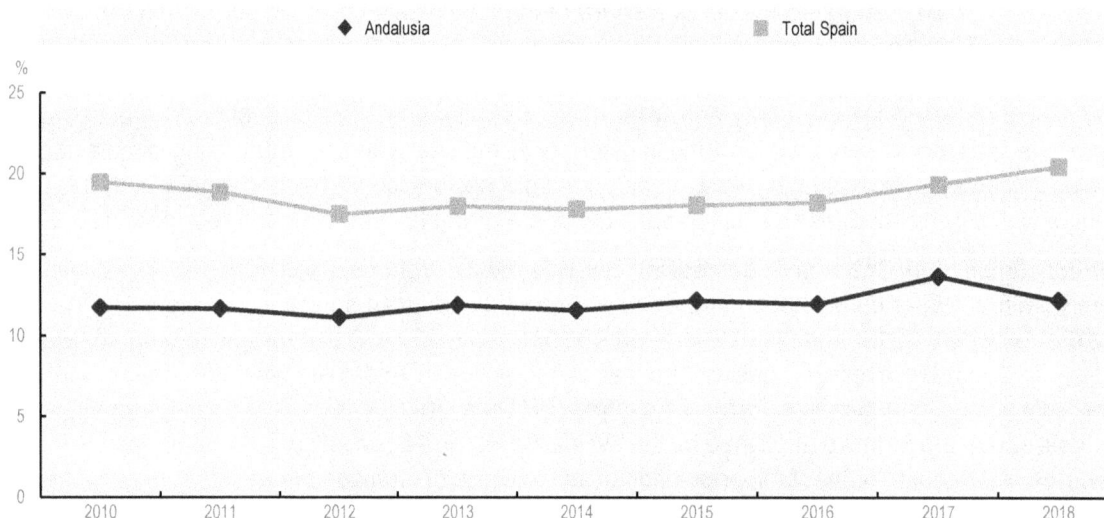

Source: INE (2019[58]), Estadísticas sobre recogida y tratamiento de residuos. Residuos urbanos: Serie 2010-2018, https://www.ine.es/jaxi/Ta bla.htm?path=/t26/e068/p01/serie/l0/&file=02003.px&L=0.

No clear trend towards reduced final energy[3] consumption can be observed for the province of Granada between 2008 and 2018. However, the municipality aims to enhance energy efficiency. (Government of Andalusia, 2019[64]). Final energy consumption has varied between 1 164.3 and 1 396.3 kilotonnes of oil equivalent annually over this period. However, the province of Granada accounted for just 9.9% of Andalusia's total energy use in 2018, with Cádiz, Málaga and Seville being the highest energy consumers. In 2018, 67.5% of the province of Granada's final energy consumption came from fossil sources (petroleum and natural gas), while 22.1% of the final energy consumed was electric. Transport – which still overwhelmingly depends on fossil fuels – and the residential sector were the main drivers of final energy consumption, accounting for 41.6% and 20.9% respectively in 2018. The municipality aims to reduce consumption through savings and efficiency campaigns in the residential sector, the implementation of the Sustainable Urban Mobility Plan 2025[4] and the use of alternative energies (Granada City Council, 2013[65]). The transition to a circular economy can contribute by promoting shared transport solutions, thus increasing efficiency and by improving energy efficiency in buildings. Further details on how the circular economy can contribute to a more sustainable Granada will be discussed in Chapter 2.

## References

CEPR (2020), *Covid Economics*, Centre for Economic Policy Research, https://cepr.org/content/covid-economics-vetted-and-real-time-papers-0 (accessed on 9 April 2021). [15]

CGCOM (2021), *CGCOM | Consejo General de Colegios de Médicos*, https://www.cgcom.es/ (accessed on 4 May 2021). [3]

Circle Economy et al. (2016), *CIRCULAR AMSTERDAM A vision and action agenda for the city and metropolitan area*, https://www.circle-economy.com/wp-content/uploads/2016/04/Circular-Amsterdam-EN-small-210316.pdf (accessed on 30 April 2019). [48]

EC (2019), *Assessment Report for the City of Granada: Creativity and Wellness, Core of the Digital Transformation in Granada Digital Cities Challenge*, European Commission. [66]

EEA (2019), *The Sustainability Transition in Europe in an Age of Demographic and Technological Change*, European Environment Agency, https://www.eea.europa.eu/publications/sustainability-transition-in-europe (accessed on 5 April 2021). [25]

EEA (2016), *More from Less - Material Resource Efficiency in Europe*, European Environment Agency. [8]

Ellen MacArthur Foundation (2019), *Introduction to the Circular Economy*. [5]

Emasagra (2020), *Agua del Grifo, Agua de Calidad*, https://www.emasagra.es/agua-del-grifo-agua-de-calidad (accessed on 9 April 2021). [61]

Emasagra (2020), *Informe de Desarrollo Sostenible*, https://www.emasagra.es/informe-de-desarrollo-sostenible (accessed on 25 January 2021). [59]

EP Data (2021), *La situación del agua en España y en el mundo*, https://www.epdata.es/datos/graficos-situacion-agua-mundo-espana/333 (accessed on 9 April 2021). [60]

FAO (2020), *Urban Food Agenda*, Food and Agriculture Organization of the United Nations, http://www.fao.org/urban-food-agenda/en/ (accessed on 30 September 2020). [9]

Forum Ambiental Foundation (2019), *Premios Ciudad Sostenible (Sustainable City Awards)*. [57]

Funcas (2021), *Indicadores Regionales*, https://www.funcas.es/textointegro/indicadores-regionales-5-enero-2021/ (accessed on 11 January 2021). [68]

Government of Andalusia (2021), *Inventory of Atmospheric Emissions in Andalusia*. [49]

Government of Andalusia (2020), *Estadística de la Red de Espacios Culturales de Andalucía*, https://www.juntadeandalucia.es/servicios/estadistica-cartografia/actividad/detalle/175086/175547.html (accessed on 12 January 2021). [28]

Government of Andalusia (2020), *Informe de Medio Ambiente en Andalucía*, http://www.juntadeandalucia.es/medioambiente/portal_web/ima/2019/iMA_2019.pdf (accessed on 9 April 2021). [62]

Government of Andalusia (2019), *Datos Energéticos de Andalucía 2018*, http://www.agenciaandaluzadelaenergia.es (accessed on 9 April 2021). [64]

Government of Andalusia (2019), *Statistics on Integrated Production in Andalusia 2019*, https://www.juntadeandalucia.es/export/drupaljda/PI%202019_3.pdf (accessed on 22 January 2021). [37]

Government of Andalusia/Granada City Council (2020), *Plan Turístico de Grandes Ciudades de Andalucía de la ciudad de Granada*, https://www.juntadeandalucia.es/organismos/turismoregeneracionjusticiayadministracionlocal/consejeria/sobre-consejeria/planes/detalle/206317.html (accessed on 15 January 2021). [29]

Government of Spain (2021), *Estadísticas de producción integrada*, https://www.mapa.gob.es/es/agricultura/estadisticas/estadistica-produccion-integrada.aspx (accessed on 22 January 2021). [36]

Government of Spain (2020), *Recovery, Transformation and Resilience Plan*, https://www.lamoncloa.gob.es/presidente/actividades/Documents/2020/07102020_PlanRecuperacion.pdf (accessed on 9 April 2021). [2]

Government of Spain (2019), *Evaluación de la calidad del aire en España*. [50]

Granada City Council (2021), "La candidatura de Granada a la Capitalidad Europea de la Cultura en 2031 inicia su andadura con el apoyo de todas las instituciones y formaciones políticas", https://www.granada.org/inet/wprensa.nsf/fa487bb870324f4fc12579b800461d1d/050e0391bf93550ec1257f0f0045d55b!OpenDocument (accessed on 12 January 2021). [31]

Granada City Council (2020), "Nace el 'skyline' verde de la ciudad de Granada, el Anillo Verde (The green "skyline" of the city of Granada)", https://www.granada.org/inet/wprensa.nsf/0284aa18655e179cc1257be5003cc7f9/a5de6a806ee30b5ec125860a003fbd09!OpenDocument (accessed on 8 January 2021). [55]

Granada City Council (2019), "El Ayuntamiento extiende a toda la ciudad la limitación de la velocidad a 30 kilómetros hora (Granada City Council extends 30 km/h speed limit to the whole city)", https://www.granada.org/inet/wprensa.nsf/0284aa18655e179cc1257be5003cc7f9/70e611af3514ce92c12583d8004022ed!OpenDocument (accessed on 19 January 2021). [56]

Granada City Council (2017), *Plan de mejora de la calidad del aire del término municipal de Granada 2017-2020 (Air Quality Improvement Plan for 2017-2020)*, https://www.granada.org/inet/wordenanz.nsf/wwalias/3DA6AC842BD8A240C1258221004B7F52 (accessed on 18 January 2021). [53]

Granada City Council (2015), *Estrategia Granada 2020: Haciendo Humano lo Urbano (EG2020): Consejo Social de la Ciudad de Granada*, https://www.granada.org/inet/consejosocial.nsf/byclave/ELRJLRR (accessed on 19 January 2021). [24]

Granada City Council (2013), *Sustainable Urban Mobility Plan*, http://www.movilidadgranada.com/pmus_index.php (accessed on 26 January 2021). [65]

Granada Ciudad de la Ciencia y la Innovación (2021), *El proyecto – Granada Ciudad de la Ciencia*, http://www.granadaciencia.es/el-proyecto/ (accessed on 19 January 2021). [32]

IFC (2020), *COVID-19's Impact on the Waste Sector*, International Finance Corporation, World Bank Group, https://www.ifc.org/wps/wcm/connect/industry_ext_content/ifc_external_corporate_site/infrastructure/resources/covid-19-and-waste-sector (accessed on 12 April 2021). [17]

IISD (2018), "Estimating employment effects of the circular economy", Background Note, International Institute for Sustainable Development, https://www.iisd.org/system/files/publications/employment-effects-circular-economy.pdf?q=sites/default/files/publications/employment-effects-circular-economy.pdf. [47]

ILO (2019), *World Employment and Social Outlook – Trends 2019*, International Labour Organization. [46]

INE (2021), *Cifras oficiales de población resultantes de la revisión del Padrón municipal a 1 de enero*, Instituto Nacional de Estadística, https://www.ine.es/jaxiT3/Datos.htm?t=2911#!tabs-tabla (accessed on 19 January 2021). [23]

INE (2021), *Población por capitales de provincia y sexo*, Instituto Nacional de Estadística, https://www.ine.es/jaxiT3/Tabla.htm?t=2911&L=0 (accessed on 12 January 2021). [20]

INE (2021), *Población por comunidades y ciudades autónomas y sexo*, Instituto Nacional de Estadística, https://www.ine.es/jaxiT3/Tabla.htm?t=2853&L=0 (accessed on 12 January 2021). [19]

INE (2020), *Indicadores de Estructura de la Población*, Instituto Nacional de Estadística, https://www.ine.es/dynt3/inebase/index.htm?padre=2077&capsel=2077 (accessed on 14 January 2021). [22]

INE (2019), *Estadísticas sobre recogida y tratamiento de residuos. Residuos urbanos: Serie 2010-2018*, Instituto Nacional de Estadística, https://www.ine.es/jaxi/Tabla.htm?path=/t26/e068/p01/serie/l0/&file=02003.px&L=0. [58]

Institute of Statistics and Cartography of Andalusia (2021), *Padrón Municipal de Habitantes. Cifras oficiales de población municipal*, https://www.juntadeandalucia.es/institutodeestadisticaycartografia/badea/operaciones/consulta/anual/6675?CodOper=b3_128&codConsulta=6675 (accessed on 12 January 2021). [21]

Institute of Statistics and Cartography of Andalusia (2021), *Tasa municipal de desempleo*, http://www.juntadeandalucia.es/institutodeestadisticaycartografia/sima/info.htm?f=j11 (accessed on 19 January 2021). [40]

Institute of Statistics and Cartography of Andalusia (2018), *Andalucía pueblo a pueblo - Fichas Municipales*, https://www.juntadeandalucia.es/institutodeestadisticaycartografia/sima/ficha.htm?mun=1808 7 (accessed on 7 April 2021). [42]

Intelligent Cities Challenge (2020), *Granada, Spain*, https://www.intelligentcitieschallenge.eu/cities/granada (accessed on 8 January 2021). [67]

Ministry of Employment and Social Security (2020), *Informe del Mercado de Trabajo de Granada*, https://www.sepe.es/HomeSepe/que-es-el-sepe/comunicacion-institucional/publicaciones/publicaciones-oficiales/listado-pub-mercado-trabajo/informe-mercadotrabajo-estatal-general.html (accessed on 11 January 2021). [34]

Ministry of Health (2021), *Coronavirus Update*, https://www.mscbs.gob.es/fr/profesionales/saludPublica/ccayes/alertasActual/nCov/situacion Actual.htm (accessed on 4 May 2021). [4]

Ministry of Health, Consumer Affairs and Social Welfare (2021), *New Coronavirus Disease, COVID-19*, https://www.mscbs.gob.es/profesionales/saludPublica/ccayes/alertasActual/nCov/situacionAc tual.htm (accessed on 9 April 2021). [1]

National Public Employment Service (2020), *Informe del Mercado de Trabajo Granada. Datos 2019*. [41]

OECD (2021), *OECD Statistics*, OECD, Paris, https://stats.oecd.org/ (accessed on 10 February 2021). [51]

OECD (2021), *Unemployment Rate - OECD Data*, OECD, Paris, https://data.oecd.org/unemp/unemployment-rate.htm (accessed on 9 April 2021). [38]

OECD (2020), "Cities policy responses", *OECD Policy Responses to Coronavirus (COVID-19)*, OECD, Paris, https://www.oecd.org/coronavirus/policy-responses/cities-policy-responses-fd1053ff/. [16]

OECD (2020), *OECD Survey on Circular Economy in Cities and Regions*, OECD, Paris. [52]

OECD (2020), *The Circular Economy in Cities and Regions: Synthesis Report*, OECD Urban Studies, OECD Publishing, Paris, https://dx.doi.org/10.1787/10ac6ae4-en. [6]

OECD (2012), *OECD Environmental Outlook to 2050: The Consequences of Inaction*, OECD Publishing, Paris, https://dx.doi.org/10.1787/9789264122246-en. [11]

OECD/EC (2020), *Cities in the World: A New Perspective on Urbanisation*, OECD Urban Studies, OECD Publishing, Paris, https://dx.doi.org/10.1787/d0efcbda-en. [7]

Official Association of Biologists of Andalusia (2021), "Andalucía reutiliza 4,8% de su agua residual tratada, por debajo de la media", https://andaluciainformacion.es/andalucia/959230/andalucia-reutiliza-48-de-su-agua-residual-tratada-por-debajo-de-la-media/ (accessed on 9 April 2021). [63]

onGranada (2018), "onGranada consigue la calificación europea de Digital Innovation Hub", https://www.ongranada.com/ongranada-consigue-la-calificacion-europea-digital-innovation-hub/ (accessed on 12 January 2021).   [33]

Provincial Council of Granada (2021), "Diputación comienza en Gójar las mediciones para el diagnóstico de calidad del aire en el área metropolitana de Granada (The Provincial Council begins in Gójar the measurements for the diagnosis of air quality in the metropolitan area of Granada)", https://www.dipgra.es/amplia-actualidad/noticias-inicio/diputacion-comienza-gojar-mediciones-diagnostico-calidad-del-aire-area-metropolitana-granada (accessed on 22 January 2021).   [54]

Romano, O. (2020), "Resilient people and places: Why cities should embrace the circular economy to shape our post-COVID-19 future", OECD, Paris, http://www.oecd-forum.org/posts/resilient-people-and-places-why-cities-should-embrace-the-circular-economy-to-shape-our-post-covid-19-future (accessed on 29 July 2020).   [14]

Spanish Public Employment Service (2021), *Estadísticas por municipios (paro registrado y contratos)*, https://sepe.es/HomeSepe/que-es-el-sepe/estadisticas/datos-estadisticos.html (accessed on 18 January 2021).   [39]

Spanish Public Employment Service (2020), *Estudio Prospectivo de las Actividades Económicas Relacionadas con la Economía Circular en España*, https://www.sepe.es/HomeSepe/que-es-el-sepe/comunicacion-institucional/noticias/detalle-noticia.html?folder=/2020/Noviembre/&detail=estudio-prospectivo-de-las-actividades-economicas-relacionadas-con-la-economia-circular-en-espana (accessed on 18 January 2021).   [44]

Spanish Public Employment Service (2020), "Prospective study of economic activities related to the circular economy in Spain", https://www.sepe.es/HomeSepe/que-es-el-sepe/comunicacion-institucional/noticias/detalle-noticia.html?folder=/2020/Noviembre/&detail=estudio-prospectivo-de-las-actividades-economicas-relacionadas-con-la-economia-circular-en-espana (accessed on 9 April 2021).   [43]

UNEP (2020), *Working with the Environment to Protect People: Covid-19 Response*, United Nations Environment Programme, https://www.unep.org/resources/working-environment-protect-people-covid-19-response (accessed on 12 April 2021).   [18]

UNEP (2013), *UNEP-DTIE Sustainable Consumption and Production Branch*, United Nations Environment Programme.   [10]

UNEP/IWSA (2015), *Global Waste Management Outlook*, United Nations Environment Programme.   [12]

UNESCO (2021), *Granada*, United Nations Educational, Scientific and Cultural Organization, https://en.unesco.org/creative-cities/node/19 (accessed on 12 January 2021).   [30]

Unicaja (2019), *Informe Anual del Sector Agrario en Andalucía 2018*, http://www.analistaseconomicos.com (accessed on 22 January 2021).   [35]

University of Granada (2020), *Anexo estadístico 2019-2020*, https://secretariageneral.ugr.es/pages/memorias/academica/20192020/estadistica (accessed on 11 January 2021).   [27]

University of Granada (2020), "La UGR es la universidad andaluza mejor posicionada en el ranking mundial CWUR, y la sexta de España", https://www.ugr.es/universidad/noticias/ugr-universidad-andaluza-mejor-posicionada-ranking-mundial-cwur (accessed on 5 April 2021).  [26]

World Bank (2010), *World Development Report 2010*, World Bank, Washington, DC, http://dx.doi.org/10.1596/978-0-8213-7987-5.  [13]

WRAP/Green Alliance (2015), *Employment and the Circular Economy: Job Creation in a More Resource Efficient Britain*, https://circulareconomy.europa.eu/platform/sites/default/files/britain_employment_and_ce.pdf.  [45]

## Notes

[1] Calculated as the mean annual outdoor PM2.5 concentration weighted by population living in the relevant area, that is, the concentration level, expressed in µg/m$^3$, to which a typical resident is exposed throughout a year.

[2] Alhendín, Armilla, Cájar, Cenes de la Vega, Cúllar Vega, Churriana de la Vega, Gójar, Huétor Vega, La Zubia, Las Gabias, Ogíjares, Otura, Pinos Genil and Pulianas.

[3] Final energy measures all energy supplied to the final end users (households, agriculture, industry, services, etc.) for all energy uses (Government of Andalusia, 2019[64]).

[4] See http://www.movilidadgranada.com/pmus_index.php.

# 2 Towards the circular economy in Granada, Spain

This chapter analyses existing initiatives across levels of government related to the circular economy. Applying the 3Ps framework, *people, policies and places*, the chapter also identifies actors, policies and co-operation tools across urban and rural areas that can foster the circular economy.

## The circular economy agenda at the national and subnational levels

The transition towards the circular economy in Spain takes place under the framework of the National Circular Economy Strategy (*España Circular 2030*), which sets goals for 2030. In June 2020, the Council of Ministers approved the Spanish Circular Economy Strategy (España Circular 2030), which lays the foundations for overcoming the linear economy and promoting a new production and consumption model in Spain. The strategy sets targets for 2030 including, among others, the reduction of national consumption of materials by 30%, the improvement of water use efficiency by 10% and a 15% cut in waste generation compared to 2010 levels, which would keep greenhouse gas (GHG) emissions from the waste sector below 10 million tonnes in 2030. The strategy highlights the importance of taking advantage of the opportunities offered by the circular economy to develop a Spanish industry focused on recycling. It identifies six priority sectors: construction; agri-food, fisheries and forestry; industry; consumer goods; tourism; and textiles and clothing. The implementation of the strategy in Spain is co-ordinated by three main bodies: i) an inter-ministerial commission with the ministries involved; ii) a Working Group of the Coordination Commission on Waste with the autonomous communities and local entities; and iii) a Circular Economy Council with economic and social agents. The adoption of the Spanish Circular Economy Strategy was foreseen in the Declaration of Climate and Environmental Emergency approved in January 2020 and is consistent with the draft Climate Change and Energy Transition Act (Box 2.1) (Government of Spain, 2020[1]).

---

### Box 2.1. Towards a new Law on Climate Change and Energy Transition of Spain

The first draft of the Law on Climate Change and Energy Transition, aiming for Spain to achieve emission neutrality by 2050, was approved by the Congress of Deputies on 8 April 2021. Its adoption by the Senate is pending. The law is the result of a public participation and review process by key national and subnational institutions, initiated in February 2019. It is expected to be supplemented by national energy and climate plans (NECP) that will determine precise climate objectives and targets. The first of these plans is expected to cover the period 2021-30 and design a trajectory to reduce emissions by 23% compared to 1990, increasing the percentage of renewables in gross final energy consumption to at least 42% by 2030. Regarding energy efficiency, the 2030 primary energy consumption target represents a 39.6% reduction compared to the baseline projections.

The text comprises a series of actions in relation to the promotion of energy efficiency and sustainable mobility, amongst others. It recognises the role of cities, in achieving climate objectives, thereby favouring the creation of more liveable and healthier spaces, with improved air quality. In this regard, it establishes that municipalities with more than 50 000 inhabitants will introduce mitigation measures in urban planning to reduce emissions from mobility, including the implementation of low-emission zones no later than 2023 (Article 12 of the draft law).

The draft law establishes that a percentage of the general state budget will be earmarked to contribute to climate change and energy transition objectives. Revenues from the auctioning of GHG emission allowances (at least 450 million) will also be used to meet climate change targets. Finally, the law will foresee an independent Committee of Experts on Climate Change and Energy Transition, responsible for evaluating and making recommendations on energy and climate change policies and measures.

Source: Congress of Deputies (2021[2]), *Spanish Draft Law on Climate Change and Energy Transition*, https://www.congreso.es/backoffice_doc/prensa/notas_prensa/81345_1617867418184.pdf.

---

In response to the COVID-19 crisis, Spain's Recovery, Transformation and Resilience Plan includes the ecological transition as one of the four pillars for recovery. The plan contains a total of 30 measures, including the Plan to Support the Implementation of the Spanish Circular Economy Strategy and waste regulations. The National Circular Economy Strategy (España Circular 2030) is one of the key elements of the Circular Economy Framework (*Marco de Economía Circular*), included amongst the government projects as a lever for economic recovery from the COVID-19 crisis.

At the regional level, the Government of Andalusia developed its circular economy strategy combined with a series of initiatives related to the transition:

- The 2018 Andalusian Circular Bioeconomy Strategy (*Estrategia Andaluza de Bioeconomia Circular*) focuses on the production of renewable biological resources and processes (Box 2.2).

- The 2018 Strategy for Sustainable Development 2030 (*Estrategia Andaluza de Desarrollo Sostenible 2030*) conceives the circular economy as an opportunity to achieve sustainable goals at the regional level and as a key element of the green economy (Government of Andalusia, 2018[3]).

- The 2019 Integrated Waste Plan of Andalusia: Towards a Circular Economy by 2030 (*Plan Integral de Residuos de Andalucía. Hacia una Economía Circular en el Horizonte 2030*, PIRec 2030) seeks to: i) encourage industrial symbiosis for the reuse of generated by-products; ii) analyse the efficiency of current collection systems, optimise treatment processes and carry out an evaluation of the management processes; and iii) promote the construction of recovery and disposal facilities to make Andalusia self-sufficient in the management of all of its waste (Government of Andalusia, 2019[4]).

- The 2020 Draft Circular Economy Law (*Anteproyecto de Ley de Economía Circular de Andalucía*) aims to create an appropriate regulatory framework to promote the rational use of resources, extend the useful life of products and minimise waste generation. The law is expected to be approved by 2022. Other relevant characteristics of the draft law are the implementation of a circular model to so-called "key products" (i.e. electronics and information and communication technology [ICT]; batteries and vehicles; packaging; plastics; textiles; construction and buildings; and food, water and nutrients) and of the blue circular economy to promote integrated management of the water cycle. The Andalusian Office of Circular Economy will be the administrative body in charge of implementing the law, as well as co-ordinating, advising and providing support to companies and local administrations (Government of Andalusia, 2020[5]).

Clearly communicating around the achievements and environmental, economic and social impacts of these initiatives to stakeholders and citizens will be key to their effective implementation. The monitoring framework of the Andalusian Circular Bioeconomy Strategy is not yet in place. However, one of the concrete actions of the strategy involves the design of a set of specific indicators for monitoring and evaluating the progress of the strategy.

---

### Box 2.2. Andalusian Circular Bioeconomy Strategy

Launched in 2018 with the contribution of many regional ministries and institutions,[1] the main objective of the Andalusian Circular Bioeconomy Strategy is to foster the production of renewable biological resources and processes. In particular, it aims to:

- Improve the sustainability and competitiveness of the agri-food, fisheries and forestry sectors, encouraging the use of innovative practices to promote and implement a circular economy.

- Boost the competitiveness of industries working with biological resources by promoting innovation, knowledge generation and technology transfer.

---

- Promote the reuse of resources, water, gases, nutrients and the use of waste to obtain other products or energy.
- Promote research, innovation and skills related to the bioeconomy.
- Strengthen inter-administrative co-ordination and synergies with other work plans and programmes in different fields.

The strategy sets out four pillars:

- Sustainable generation of biomass resource availability.
- Infrastructure and logistics management.
- Industrial processes for the transformation of biomass resources and industrial production capacity for bioproducts and bioenergy.
- Market development for bioproducts and bioenergy.

The strategy identifies four cross-cutting instrumental programmes for its implementation:

- Communication and public awareness of the bioeconomy.
- Promotion of research and development (R&D) for the development and expansion of the bioeconomy in Andalusia.
- Access to finance to facilitate the development of the bioeconomy.
- Co-operation, co-ordination and monitoring of the bioeconomy.

Source: Government of Andalusia (2018[6]), *Andalusian Strategy for the Circular Bioeconomy*, https://www.juntadeandalucia.es/organismos/sobre-junta/planes/detalle/155202.html.

The Provincial Council of Granada has set up awareness-raising initiatives on the circular economy but planning documents still focus on waste rather than on natural resources management. In 2020, the council organised a series of seminars on the circular economy within the framework of the European Color Circle project,[2] providing a forum for learning and exchanging successful circular practices to companies and other organisations from the province of Granada. The workshops welcomed good practices from several sectors, including agricultural production, food innovation and wastewater management. The Color Circle project foresees co-operation with other European partners from the Czech Republic, France, the Netherlands and Romania to empower local authorities, connecting them with research teams, towards the full development of the circular economy (Provincial Council of Granada, 2020[7]). Moreover, the Municipal Waste Management Programme for the Province of Granada 2014-24 includes the selective collection (mainly organic and inorganic recyclables), recovery and the establishment of mechanisms for the identification and management of other waste categories (e.g. electronic waste, used oils and batteries) (Provincial Council of Granada, 2014[8]). However, there is no mention of the transition to the circular economy in the programme.

The Provincial Council of Granada finances sustainable initiatives in the metropolitan area of Granada, which may have impacts on the circular economy in terms of waste management. The council co-ordinates the Integrated Sustainable Urban Development Strategies (EDUSI) for a total investment of EUR 31.5 million. In 2020, the municipality of Granada adhered to the strategy, aiming at implementing the EDUSI programme by 2022. Some actions included in the plan concern the extension of the network of underground containers that already exists in the city, placing two selective waste containers (glass, paper and packaging) at two points in the historic centre of Granada. This initiative aims to promote the selective collection of waste, introducing aesthetic and environmental improvements in the historic centre, while taking care of the heritage surroundings (Granada City Council, 2020[9]).

# Circular economy initiatives in Granada, Spain

Granada is taking the first steps towards the circular and low-carbon economy. In 2017, the city of Granada adhered to the Declaration of Seville, which aims to promote the circular economy in signatory cities (300 Spanish municipalities), in particular by fostering recycling (especially biowaste), preventing waste (particularly food waste), promoting eco-design and the public procurement of green products. Although not binding, the declaration represents a starting point for Spanish municipalities to take action towards the circular economy. Moreover, the city of Granada joined the Global Covenant of Mayors for Climate and Energy Europe in 2009, the world's largest alliance of cities and local governments seeking to promote and support voluntary actions to tackle climate change. For signatory cities, this commitment implies achieving a share of energy consumption from renewable sources and energy savings of at least 27%, as well as a 40% reduction in $CO_2$ emissions by 2030 (Covenant of Mayors, 2020[10]).

The water sector represented the entry point for a wider debate on the circular economy in the city. The transformation of the wastewater treatment plant into a biofactory initiated in 2015, managed by the mixed ownership company Emasagra (the Municipal Water Supply and Sanitation Company), allowed the increasing reuse of water and its transformation into energy. Compared to the previous model, the biofactory represents a new way to achieve circularity through energy generation, water reuse and recovery of waste resulting from the purification process of water. According to Emasagra, the innovation consists in: i) moving from being a big consumer of energy to producer; ii) reusing treated water rather than only purifying it and returning to the natural environment; and iii) transforming waste into resources, rather than dumping it into the landfill (see section on policies).

The most recent initiatives led by the city concern raising awareness on the circular economy. The Health, Education and Youth Municipal Department of the municipality designed in 2019 the training programme "Circular Economy and Recycling: The Solution for the Environment" for students from primary school, secondary school, and higher education (Granada City Council, 2020[11]). During the 2020/21 academic year, a total of 1 200 students from 24 educational institutions are expected to attend the programme. Moreover, by 2021, the city of Granada foresees to issue a monthly newsletter *Circular Granada* in Granada's two main newspapers, which will include the major circular economy initiatives taking place in the city. Also, the municipality provides a daily list of furniture to be deposited on the public streets for removal, so that citizens can make a reservation and collect them for reuse (Inagra, 2020[12]).

**Figure 2.1. Timeline of circular economy initiatives in the city of Granada, the province of Granada, Andalusia and Spain**

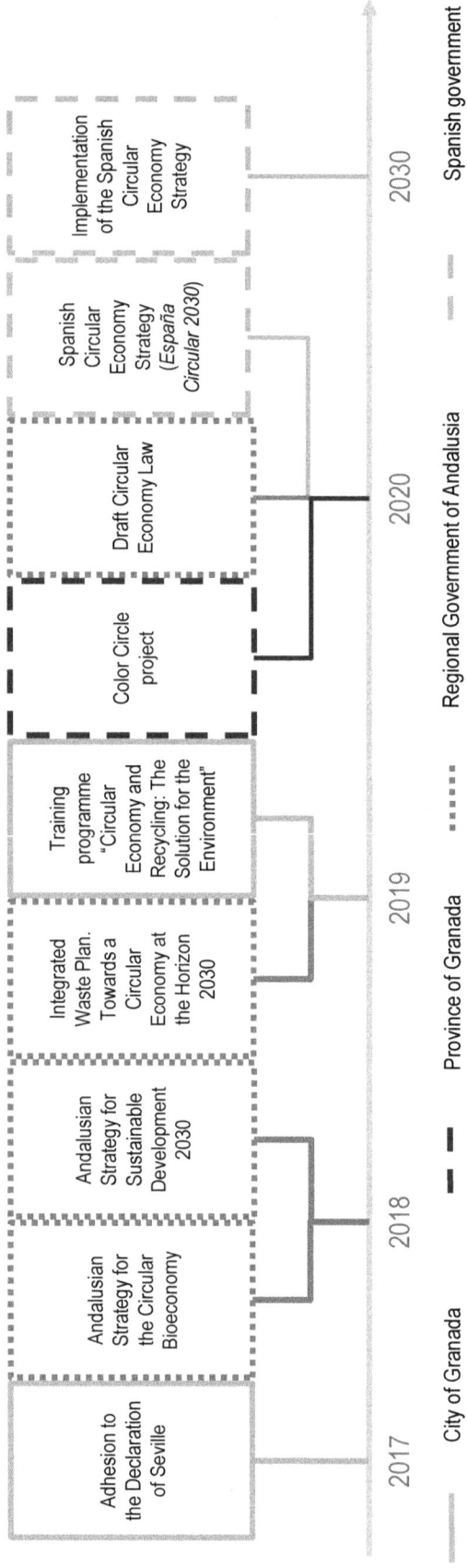

Adhesion to the Declaration of Seville

Andalusian Strategy for the Circular Bioeconomy

Andalusian Strategy for Sustainable Development 2030

Integrated Waste Plan. Towards a Circular Economy at the Horizon 2030

Training programme "Circular Economy and Recycling: The Solution for the Environment"

Color Circle project

Draft Circular Economy Law

Spanish Circular Economy Strategy (España Circular 2030)

Implementation of the Spanish Circular Economy Strategy

2017    2018    2019    2020    2030

City of Granada    Province of Granada    Regional Government of Andalusia    Spanish government

## The 3Ps analytical framework

The below section identifies opportunities for the circular economy in Granada based on the 3Ps framework "people, policies and places", set out in *The Circular Economy in Cities and Regions: Synthesis Report* (OECD, 2020[13]) on the basis of *Water Governance in Cities* (OECD, 2016[14]):

- **People**: The circular economy is a shared responsibility across levels of government and stakeholders. As such, it is key to identify the actors that can play a role in the transition and allow the needed cultural shift towards different production and consumption pathways, new business and governance models. For example, the business sector can determine the shift towards new business models (e.g. renting, reusing, sharing, etc.). Citizens, on the other hand, make constant consumption choices and can influence production.

- **Policies**: The circular economy requires a holistic and systemic approach that cuts across sectoral policies, from environmental, regional development, agricultural and industrial ones. As somebody's waste can be a resource for somebody else, the circular economy provides the opportunity to foster complementarities across policies. The variety of actors, sectors and goals makes the circular economy systemic by nature. Identifying the key sectors and possible synergies is the first step to avoid the implementation of fragmented projects over the short-medium run, due to the lack of a systemic approach.

- **Places**: Cities and regions are not isolated ecosystems but spaces for inflows and outflows of materials, resources and products, in connection with surrounding areas. Therefore, adopting a functional approach going beyond the administrative boundaries of cities is important for resource management and economic development. Linkages across urban and rural areas (e.g. related to agriculture and forest) are key to promote local production and recycling of organic residuals to be used in proximity of where they are produced, to avoid negative externalities due to transport. At the regional level, loops related to a series of economic activities (e.g. to the bioeconomy) can be closed and slowed.

This section draws from the input provided during the OECD mission to Granada on 25-28 March 2019, when more than 70 stakeholders from the private, public and not-for-profit sectors were interviewed.

### *People*

The below section identifies stakeholders that amongst others can contribute to the transition from a linear to a circular economy, such as universities, technological clusters, the Granada Chamber of Commerce and Industry and sectoral and consumer associations. The Cotec Foundation identified key actors for the circular economy transition in Spain, which are reported in Box 2.3.

---

### Box 2.3. Selected circular economy actors in Spain by Cotec

The Cotec Foundation is a non-profit organisation aiming at promoting innovation for social and economic development. In 2017, the foundation carried out a mapping of actors and practices of public and private entities. It identified large companies, small- and medium-sized enterprises (SMEs), non-profit and -governmental organisations that have implemented circular economy good practices and processes in different sectors, such as:

---

- **Waste**
  - o Anfevi: The National Association of Automatic Glass Container Manufacturing Companies has invested in R&D on sustainability and promoted the recycling of glass containers since 1980. The recent campaign "*#YoElijoVidrio*" aims at raising awareness of the importance of the reuse of glass containers in Spain.
  - o Ecoembes is a non-profit organisation (NPO) that manages the collection, sorting and recycling process of plastic packaging, cans, paper and cardboard packaging all over Spain. In 2017, Ecoembes launched the CircularLab: an innovation centre on the circular economy, which provides support to innovations in the fields of packaging and subsequent recycling.
  - o Ecotic is a non-profit organisation whose main activity is the sustainable and compliant management of waste electrical and electronic equipment (WEEE) from companies and entities, which contributes to its Collective System of Extended Producer Responsibility (SCRAP).

- **Water**
  - o CETaqua, the Water Technology Center, is a national and international non-profit foundation in charge of research, technological development and innovation in relation to the water cycle, especially the urban cycle. The founding partners of CETaqua are Aigües de Barcelona (Agbar), the Polytechnic University of Catalonia (UPC) and the Spanish National Research Council (CSIC).

- **Food and agriculture**
  - o Desarrollo Rural Cataluña Central is a co-operative dealing with agricultural practices and focusing on the creation, expansion and improvement of agri-food companies of local and organic products and on the implementation of projects that promote the green economy and especially the circular economy (e.g.: EnFoCC Project).
  - o Mercadona is Spain's largest supermarket group, with more than 1 600 shops nationwide. It will invest more than EUR 140 million by 2025 to reduce plastic by 25%, make all packaging recyclable and recycle all plastic waste.
  - o Espigoladors is a social enterprise preventing food waste and empowering people who are vulnerable to social exclusion.

- **Energy**
  - o Neoelectra is a power generation company that has been using efficient and environmentally friendly technologies such as cogeneration, biomass and biogas since 1999.

- **Health**
  - o SOLUTEX is a private organisation providing technological solutions to the pharmaceutical sector. Since its creation in 2004, Solutex has based all its operations on the circular economy model. The company has a zero-waste policy and reuses all by-products derived from the manufacturing processes. Solutex is a member of the European Technology Platform for Sustainable Chemistry and actively participates in la European public-private partnership SPIRE (Sustainable Process Industry through Resource and Energy Efficiency).
  - o TECNALIA is a private foundation focusing on innovation and technological development and providing advice to private companies to encourage sustainable and circular business models in the fields of energy, industry, transportation, construction, health and ICT.

Source: Cotec Foundation (2017[15]), *The Situation and Development of the Circular Economy in Spain.*

The University of Granada (UGR) leads several initiatives and projects addressing the circular economy or related subjects:

- Technologies for the circular economy: In 2018, the Higher School of Engineering of Roads, Canals and Ports (*Escuela Técnica Superior de Ingeniería de Caminos, Canales y Puertos*) launched a research group on "Technologies for the circular economy". The group aims to map all ongoing courses and initiatives related to the circular economy within the UGR in order to promote inter-disciplinary synergies and addresses five main areas of research: i) eco-friendly construction, focusing on new sustainable materials; ii) management and modelling of air and noise pollution; iii) planning and management for the resilient city; iv) emerging technologies for water and waste management; and v) technologies for the analysis and management of occupational hazards (University of Granada, 2019[16]).

- Circular economy and plastics: In 2019, the Faculty of Sciences of the University of Granada organised a 20-hour introductory course on the circular economy and plastics (University of Granada, 2019[17]).

- Circular economy and inclusiveness: In 2020, the University of Granada launched a project for the collection of urban waste through the installation of collection points in its facilities. The project was carried out in collaboration with a local association (ASPROGRADES), promoting the full employment of people with intellectual disabilities (UGR, 2020[18]).

- SDG Debates (*Ciclo de Debates ODS*): Launched by the University of Granada in 2020, the debates seek to reflect on the implementation of the United Nations 2030 Agenda. These debates included a specific session on the circular economy (UGR, 2020[19]).

- "Debates of Granada" (*Debates de Granada*) on urban planning: In 2018, the Department of Urban Planning and Land Management and the Area of Architectural Composition of the University of Granada launched "Debates of Granada" to discuss urban planning strategies adopted in different Spanish cities and how to achieve a green future for Granada, among other topics. The debates involve actors such as the university, the private sector, especially the tourism and hospitality sectors, and the municipality of Granada (Debates de Granada, 2018[20]). "Debates of Granada" raised the need for a pact for sustainability that involves public and private institutions, employers, professional associations and social groups. Some inspirational models for the group are superblocks (*Supermanza*)[1] implemented in the Spanish cities of Barcelona and Vitoria[2] (Box 2.4). Existing initiatives contributing to making Granada a smart and green city can be further developed to create collaboration across universities and stakeholders on the circular economy. For example, the programme Granada Collaborates (*Granada Colabora*) supports collaborations across businesses based in the province of Granada and the University of Granada. In 2018, *Granada Colabora* identified 35 companies in the province to establish collaborations with the university (University of Granada, 2018[21]). There is potential to develop future collaborations around the circular economy.

### Box 2.4. The Superblocks system in Barcelona and Vitoria, Spain

Superblocks are urban cells of approximately 400 by 400 meters that allow vehicles to circulate along the perimeter roads, while internal streets are reserved for pedestrians and, under special conditions, for resident vehicles, services, emergencies as well as loading and unloading activities. The is to limit the presence of private vehicles in the public space and return it to the citizen.

The city of Vitoria was the first Spanish city to apply this concept. Eight years into the project, the number of private car users decreased from 36.6% in 2006 to 24% in 2014; bicycle use increased by 10%, accounting for 13% of total mobility in 2014, and public transport experienced a 100% increase in the number of users. This change in transport patterns led to a 14.7% reduction in GHGs generated by mobility.

Barcelona, Spain, launched in 2013 a pilot programme of superblocks in five areas of the city, located in the districts of Camp d'en Grassot, Eixample, Horta, Les Corts and Sant Martí. The model seeks to respond to the scarcity of green spaces, the high levels of pollution, the high rate of environmental noise, accidents and sedentary lifestyles. The design of these car-free spaces led to the creation of a network of green hubs and squares where pedestrians have priority. Following the successful implementation of these experimental small-scale initiatives, the superblock programme is set to become the street transformation model for the entire city. Following Barcelona City Council's analysis of the impacts on the city in terms of citizen flows and mobility, neighbourhood facilities and green spaces, the extension of the superblock programme to the whole of the city has been estimated as having the potential to prevent around 667 premature deaths from air pollution annually (Mueller et al., 2020). Superblocks have already been approved or designed in other Spanish cities, such as A Coruña, El Prat, Ferrol and Viladecans.

Source: Spanish Environment Congress, (2016[22]), "La supermanzana viaja desde Vitoria y Barcelona hasta Nueva York", http://www.conama2016.org/web/es/prensa/noticias/la-supermanzana-viaja-desde-vitoria-y-barcelona-hasta-nueva-york.html; Barcelona Urban Ecology Agency (2021[23]), *Superblocks*, http://www.bcnecologia.net/es/modelo-conceptual/supermanzana; Barcelona City Council (2021[24]), *Barcelona Superblock: New Stage*, https://ajuntament.barcelona.cat/superilles/en/; Mueller et al. (2020[25]) , Changing the urban design of cities for health: The superblock model, https://www.sciencedirect.com/science/article/pii/S0160412019315223 .

Granada's technological and sector-specific clusters support innovation and circular business. As business networks, these clusters allow cross-fertilisation across companies towards circular business models, promote practice exchanges and capacity building and contribute to technical innovation in different sectors, including water, waste and bioeconomy, among others. Some examples are:

- OnGranada technological cluster: Created in 2014, as an initiative of the Granada Business Confederation, the cluster is formed by private and public sector members (municipal, provincial and regional governments) alongside the University of Granada, the Granada Chamber of Commerce and Industry, and ICT business associations and unions. Businesses within the cluster apply measures aiming to reuse waste and increase resource efficiency, such as: reintroducing purified water from cancer medical care procedures into the water network; optimising the use of water in plant cultivation and drip irrigation; or seeking to recover waste from olive cultivation to convert it into biofuel. OnGranada fosters collaboration between large companies and start-ups in its network. In 2020, the cluster, in collaboration with the International Urban Cooperation (IUC) programme,[3] organised webinars on the circular economy, focusing on blockchains (IUC, 2020[26]).

- The Granada Health Technology Park (PTS) is another key actor driving Granada's technology and innovation. The PTS provides teaching, research and business development services to companies working in the pharmaceutical, health sciences, healthcare and food industries. The Andalusian Biotechnology Cluster, through its specialised unit Andalusia BioRegion operates in the PTS. It promotes biotechnology as a catalyst for social welfare and the development of the Andalusian economy, focusing on agro-biotechnology, environmental science and renewable energy. Some examples of the products developed in the cluster are the production of bioethanol and biodiesel, bioherbicides and organic nutrient products (PTS Granada, 2021[27]). The PTS, alongside the municipality, the University of Granada, the five centres of the Higher Council for Scientific Research, the Granada Business Confederation and the Delegation of Economy and Innovation of Andalusia (*Delegación de Economía e Innovación de la Junta de Andalucía*) are part of the Bureau of Science (*Mesa por la Ciencia*), created in 2017 after the Spanish Ministry of Economy, Industry and Competitiveness recognised Granada as a City of Science and Innovation. The group fosters the promotion of scientific, technological and innovation culture in the city, through the organisation of seminars and the representation of the city in international fora. One of the latest seminars of 2019, "Nutrition Made in Granada", focused on food and sustainable packing (Granada Ciudad de la Ciencia y la Innovación, 2019[28]). Considering the goals of this group, which include raising awareness on the scientific progress made in the city of Granada, the Bureau of Science can have a role in promoting future circular economy activities in Granada.
- The Sustainable Construction Cluster of Andalusia (CSA), promoted by the Provincial Council of Granada in 2014, gathers associations of constructors, banks, the UGR, construction material producers and members of the municipal, provincial and regional governments. The cluster meets four times a year and offers educational activities to its members. Construction companies based in Granada are increasingly recovering material from construction and demolition waste (CSA, 2021[29]).

The Granada Chamber of Commerce and Industry promotes awareness-raising activities on the circular economy. Breakfasts on the circular economy transition have been organised to raise awareness amongst companies. The chamber is also managing the European Regional Development Fund (ERDF) to improve business competitiveness and the green economy. It is also promoting the creation of a platform for secondary products (including waste) and mapping the location of the different participating companies to create new synergies.

Sectoral and consumer associations and some private sector stakeholders are taking steps towards pro-environmental actions that can be relevant for the transition towards the circular economy. The Confederation of Tourism and Hospitality of Granada, representing 800 businesses at the local and provincial levels, is planning to grant certificates for companies aiming to improve and evidence their commitment to sustainable development. The association is working on the development of a series of indicators to evaluate companies' performance, addressing different topics such as $CO_2$ emission reduction, the use of renewable energy sources, energy efficiency, water and waste management and the purchase of local products, among others (La Huella Verde Granada, 2021[30]). The Consumers' Union of Granada (UCA-UCE), in collaboration with NPO Ecoembes, has been developing municipal workshops on recycling. The workshops address several themes, such as the reduction of waste generated or the reuse and exploration of new uses of materials once they have lost their properties (Ecoembes, 2015[31]).

## *Policies*

All sectors are concerned in a circular economy but some have higher potential. Often, the circular economy in cities and regions is understood as synonymous with waste recycling but it goes beyond that. Making a sector "circular" implies rethinking value chains and production and consumption processes. According to OECD (2020[13]), for 40 surveyed cities and regions, the waste sector is key to their transition towards a circular economy (98%), followed by the built environment (75%), land use and spatial planning

(70%), food and beverages and water and sanitation (65%) (Figure 2.2). Below, specific attention will be given to those sectors more prominently highlighted in discussions with various stakeholders in the city of Granada, such as waste, water, urban mobility, tourism and the built environment (Table 2.1). This description does not aim to be exhaustive of the sectors that can contribute to the circular economy transition. However, it provides an overview of those activities that hold high potential in the city. This is key to signal an existing interest from "do-ers" to transition from a linear to a circular economy, in shared responsibility with the local governments, and to foresee coherent policies in the future.

For cities and regions, the circular economy can be defined as a guiding framework whereby: services (e.g. from water to waste and energy) are provided making efficient use of natural resources as primary materials and optimising their reuse; economic activities are planned and carried out in a way to close, slow and narrow loops across value chains; and infrastructures are designed and built to avoid linear lock-in (e.g. district heating, smart grid, etc.) (OECD, 2020[13]). "Circularity" implies that any output can be an input for something else within and across sectors. It aims to: make products and goods last longer through better design; produce goods using secondary and reusable materials, and renewable energy, while reducing atmospheric emissions; produce and distribute products locally and consume them in a conscious and sustainable manner; and transform waste into a resource. According to the OECD Principles on Urban Policy (OECD, 2019[32]), the circular economy is a means to encourage more efficient use of resources and more sustainable consumption and production patterns in large, intermediary and small cities, including at the neighbourhood level. This will require a combination of national and local urban policies.

**Figure 2.2. Share of sectors included in circular economy initiatives in 40 cities**

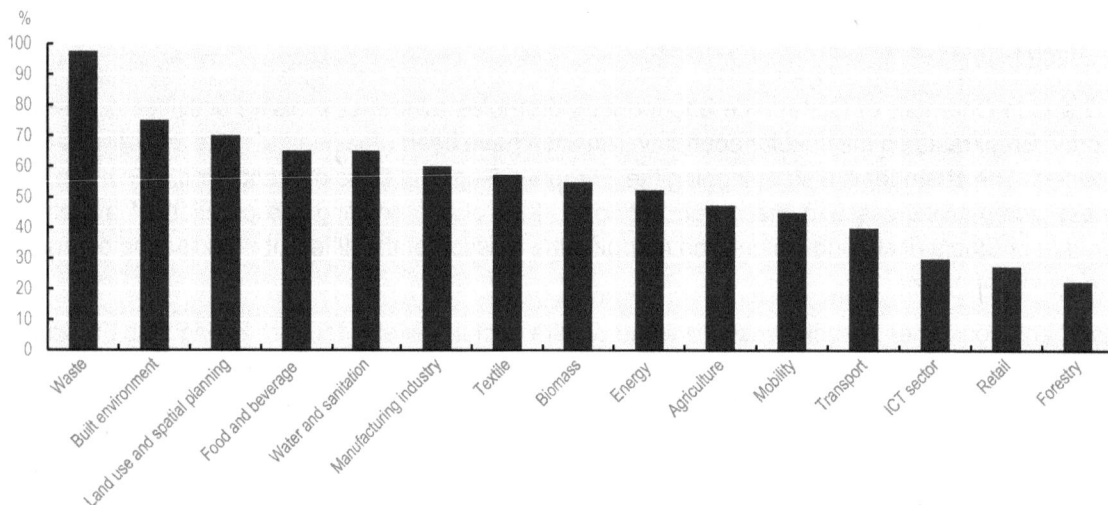

Note: Results based on a sample of 40 respondents that selected sectors responding to the question: "Which sectors are included in your city/region circular economy initiative?".
Source: OECD (2020[13]), *The Circular Economy in Cities and Regions: Synthesis Report*, https://doi.org/10.1787/10ac6ae4-en.

**Table 2.1. The potential of the circular economy in Granada per sector**

| Scope | Sector | Objectives | Activities |
|---|---|---|---|
| Services | Waste | Applying circular economy principles to waste management consists of making the most of resource use to avoid waste production and transform waste into resource. | • Prevent waste generation<br>• Promote separate collection.<br>• Apply discounts on waste taxes.<br>• Use digital tools and data for waste tracking. |
| | Water | The water cycle is circular by nature. It allows for efficient water use, water reuse and transformation of waste water into energy and materials. | • Reduce water use in the production cycles (e.g. freeing up quality resources for necessary uses and minimising water demand).<br>• Reuse of wastewater for energy production/biogas.<br>• Ensure more sustainable water flows (e.g. reducing the net discharge to natural systems).<br>• Recover materials from wastewater treatment (e.g. facilitating the recycling of nutrients for agricultural use).<br>• Use of rain and grey water.<br>• Use of regenerated water for irrigation. |
| | Urban mobility | Circularity in urban mobility aims at reducing energy consumption and limit pollution, cause of negative effects on environment, health and quality of life. | • Promote active mobility.<br>• Boost the attractiveness of public transport.<br>• Widen sustainable transportation options.<br>• Promote shared mobility options and electric vehicles. |
| Economic activities | Tourism | The tourism sector can benefit from the circular economy by closing loops in the food and hospitality sector, and by making an efficient use of water, energy and land. | • Reduce single-use furniture and especially plastic. packaging, disposable cutlery, plates and glasses.<br>• Apply circular principles in the business models of hotels (e.g. repair and reuse of beds, "product-as-a-service" schemes).<br>• Contract rental services (e.g. for specific types of furniture and laundry).<br>• Practice joint purchase and bundle of waste streams for useful applications.<br>• Use replaceable items and refurbish them by using recycled material.<br>• Prevent food waste (e.g. replacing buffet by *a la carte schemes*, selling food at a low price on platforms and donating it to food banks).<br>• Support of local food production chains. |
| Infrastructures | Built environment | Infrastructure following circular economy principles avoids linear locks-in, by making efficient use of resources, reusing material, and repurposing buildings if need be. | • Planning: Consider the entire life cycle of the building to reuse materials.<br>• Design: Take into account the material choice, reduce water and energy consumption in buildings and minimise waste.<br>• Construction: Identify sustainable and reusable materials for constructions.<br>• Operation: Use alternative energy sources and embedded technologies in buildings to enhance resource efficiency.<br>• End life: Reuse waste material produced and repurpose buildings, if need be. |

Source: Europe Direct, *European Funding in the Circular Economy*, www.europadirectogranada.eu/financiacion-europea/; and own elaboration based on OECD (2020[13]), *The Circular Economy in Cities and Regions: Synthesis Report*, https://doi.org/10.1787/10ac6ae4-en.

## Waste

In Granada, waste management performance has scarcely changed over the last few years in terms of household waste generation, reflecting the need for further efforts to improve outcomes in terms of preventing waste generation, as well as a separate collection. The city set up measures to favour separate collection, for instance by increasing the accessibility and the number of bins for different types of materials.

The number of these bins for packaging (798 bins), glass (708) and paper (688) increased by over 70% between 2012 and 2017 (Granada City Council, 2021[33]). There are also collection points for clothes, batteries and oil (181, 80 and 45 respectively). However, separate waste collection has only increased by 4% between 2004 and 2019, reaching 12% in 2019. The municipality is responsible for the collection, transport and treatment of organic waste, which is carried out through a concession agreement by the local waste company Inagra (20% municipal, 80% privately owned). The management of other categories of waste is carried out by different companies: Ecoembes for packaging; Recisur for paper and cardboard; and Ecovidrio for glass (Granada City Council, 2021[34]). The collection of unsorted waste is transferred daily by Inagra to the Alhendín treatment plant managed by the Provincial Council of Granada. Plastic paper and cardboard waste and glass waste are collected by Inagra and transported directly to authorised companies dedicated to their treatment. Once the different waste streams are treated, they are transformed into new products: plastics are used to produce swings in public spaces; construction pallets are being transformed into garden furniture; oil is used for biodiesel; glass and cardboard go to the integrated management system (Granada City Council, 2021[34]).

The city of Granada is working on the design of the future collection system. Thanks to the two underground compactors installed in the historical centre by the municipality of Granada in 2019, waste collector trucks have reduced their number of trips to two weekly. The municipality of Granada will issue a call for the cleaning and waste collection contract for the next 15 years (Granada City Council, 2021[35]). The new contract will include the following components: i) the implementation of a new line for the selective collection of organic and residual waste, which will require an investment of EUR 2 million; ii) the purchase of more than 9 000 containers for the implementation of selective collection in the Albaicín and city centre areas; and iii) a comprehensive renewal of machinery under sustainability criteria with electric or gas-powered equipment and trucks. The current contract with Inagra, in force since 1970, expired at the end of 2020 and has been exceptionally extended (Granada City Council, 2021[34]). To ensure the efficient management of waste separation and the quality of organic waste, Granada plans to provide users with a key or an application to unlock the container and create incentives (e.g. exemptions or benefits for municipal activities) to increase separation in the city (Granada City Council, 2020[36]).

The current waste fee does not cover the full cost of the service, nor does it help further prevent waste production. The waste collection fee in Granada, which does not cover the full cost of the service, consists of a fixed amount that is determined according to the nature and location of the household or business premises.[4] The city foresees the design of a fee that would reflect the actual waste produced per household. It will take into account other considerations such as the nature of the household, the quantity and the specific characteristics of the waste and the system required for its collection and treatment. In addition, the municipality of Granada exempts categories of households below a threshold of minimum income from paying the waste fee. Businesses in sectors such as hospitality, hotels or food and beverage pay according to the size of the premises (Granada City Council, 2019[37]).

While the waste sector is key to the transition from a linear to a circular economy, many cities, including Granada, focus on the downstream processes based on recycling and less on the upstream processes in relation to preventing waste. For this to happen, a series of incentives, economic instruments and adequate regulation should be put in place for private operators and individuals. These include removing harmful subsidies, providing risk-sharing financial instruments (European Union, 2019[38]) but also applying incentivising schemes for separate collection, such as the pay-as-you-throw system or differentiated tariffs. Many stakeholders (OECD, 2020[13]) flag uncertainty around the concept of waste and how materials can be reinserted into production processes when they are still reusable but, by law, qualified as "waste". In addition, roles and responsibility in the sector are highly fragmented, creating overlaps, gaps and mismanagement.

*Water*

In Granada, the emerging focus on the transition to the circular economy has been led by the water sector. The city of Granada, through the public-private water utility company, Emasagra, transformed the concept of a wastewater treatment plant into a biofactory by producing energy and new materials. The biofactory has three main objectives: i) reducing the consumption of materials to reuse water in order to recover materials (e.g. cellulose, etc.); ii) achieving 0% waste to landfill by recovering materials with high added value; and iii) producing green energy for the plant, both through self-consumption and renewable energy. In 2019, the biofactory almost reached its 100% energy self-sufficiency goal and 99% of waste valorisation. A total of 18.91 million m³ of treated water had been reused for irrigation and the maintenance of the minimum ecological flow of the local Genil River. In addition, of the 16 525 metric tonnes of fresh sludge material produced in the biofactory in 2019, 14.3% was reused for compost and 85.7% for direct application in the agricultural sector (OECD, 2020[13]). In recognition of the efforts made to reduce its GHG emissions, in 2021, the Ministry for the Ecological Transition and Demographic Challenge awarded Emasagra the environmental label Calculate + Reduce + Compensate (*Calculo + Reduzco + Compenso*) (Hidralia, 2021[39]).

The city of Granada can further explore the potential of the circular economy in the water sector, coherently with the national framework (Box 2.5). According to the results of the OECD (2020[13]), a total of 66% of circular economy initiatives reported from surveyed cities and regions, focus on the water and sanitation sector, after the waste sector (78%). In the water sector, circular economy practices can help improve environmental quality, while generating business opportunities and enhancing social well-being (Cotec Foundation, 2017[15]). Managing water in a circular way implies:

- Reducing the use of water in the production cycles, freeing up quality resources for necessary uses (supply) and minimising net water demand, reducing pressure on natural systems.

- Ensuring more sustainable water flows, reducing the net discharge to natural systems, thus decreasing pollution load and its effects on natural ecosystems.

- Reusing water for specific purposes taking into account the effects on health and the environment and making available resources that generally require less energy than other sources such as marine desalination or inter-basin transfers.

- Generating energy and recovering a wide variety of materials from wastewater treatment, such as facilitating the recycling of nutrients for agricultural use, with consequent economic benefits (reduced need for agricultural fertilisers, reduced need for tertiary treatment in wastewater management) and environmental benefits (reduced ecological footprint associated with agricultural fertilisers).

Communication around water reuse is fundamental to optimise this practice. For example, in Valladolid, Spain, together with the public service provider AQUAVALL, the city has reduced citizen use in the last decades from 450 to 230 l/day, mostly as a result of awareness-raising campaigns. The city has also upgraded water infrastructure to control losses and recover waste resources, such as fertilisers from sewage sludge, and to extend the life cycle of assets. The Public Utilities Board (PUB), Singapore's national water agency, designed an initiative to transform Singapore's waterways and waterbodies beyond their traditional functions of drainage, flood control and water storage into scenic waterscapes and focal community points. To encourage the co-creation of ABC Waters projects, PUB engaged the community from the early stages of project development to ensure that the sites were designed based on the preferences of the community, kept them updated about project progress, and worked with them to make the sites more meaningful to the community (OECD, 2016[14]).

Improving the circularity of water through reuse can have positive effects to tackle urban flooding. The city of Granada is the third most exposed area to flooding in the Guadalquivir Basin with the Granada Health Technology Park (PTS) the area with the highest flooding risk in the city. Therefore, Granada could explore opportunities for the implementation of sustainable urban drainage systems (SUDS). The application of such systems allows the use of drainage water for other purposes, keeping the water in the urban space longer than traditional drainage systems and minimising impacts such as flooding. For example, building flood parks might result in increased reuse rates, greater urban or peri-urban water use and more efficient flood management.

The generation of water resources could be used for irrigation of agricultural areas in the surrounding area or to refill the Vega de Granada aquifer (Transecto, 2020[40]; Granada City Council, 2019[41]). The use of wastewater through secondary treatment is a common practice in Granada but the necessity and the economic feasibility of advancing into tertiary water treatment processes to irrigate green crops is under debate. Accordingly to the literature, tertiary treatment contains more chemicals than secondary processing; however, it can make the water suitable for agricultural, industrial and drinking water supply needs. Nevertheless, considering the high energy consumption and the lack of economic feasibility of tertiary treatment, an alternative could be the use of groundwater, which may be cheaper and easily accessible (Sahuquillo Herráiz, 2009[42]).

---

### Box 2.5. The key role of water reuse in the transition to the circular economy in Spain

Water reuse and increased efficiency are crucial in a country like Spain, one of the driest in Europe and projected to be one of the driest in the world by 2040. Climate change will further reduce water availability: by 2030, it is expected that water inputs will decrease on average between 5% and 14% in Spain. By 2060, under a scenario of a 2.5 °C temperature increase and an 8% decrease in rainfall, a global reduction in water resources of 17% is expected on average for the peninsula, together with an increase in their inter-annual variability. These changes will be more extreme in the southern half of Spain (Iglesias, Estrela and Gallart, 2005[43]).

Currently, reused water can only serve agricultural purposes, so strengthening legislative frameworks to expand allowed uses is required. In parallel, opportunities for greater water efficiency include agricultural efficiency measures, reducing the number of illegal wells and investing in infrastructure maintenance to limit leaks. However, important financial, capacity and regulatory gaps stand in the way of achieving greater water use efficiency and dealing with climate change adaptation.

Water reuse is one of the main lines of action of Spain's Circular Economy Strategy (España Circular 2030), approved by the Council of Ministers in June 2020. The Spanish government aims to increase water efficiency by 10% by 2030 and is looking for ways to measure progress by monitoring the targets and actions included in the Action Plan 2022. Four main water reuse-related actions are planned:

- Update the regulatory frameworks on wastewater and sewage sludge reuse to guarantee that all sludge is treated in an appropriate and safe way.
- Support irrigation projects including wastewater reuse.
- Include water reuse actions in river basin management plans.
- Promote research to establish the minimum quality criteria required for water reuse.

However, in the context of significant technological development, a number of legal and social perception barriers might limit the widespread adoption of wastewater reuse. In particular, he regulatory framework needs to be adapted to the available technological innovations; and communication around the socio-economic and environmental benefits of water reuse is needed, to overcome the negative social perception of reused water. Finally, a more integrated approach to the circular water economy is needed. Isolated application of reclaimed water reuse actions may lead to unintended effects as the potential benefits of reuse could be neutralised by an overall increase in water demand. As such, reclaimed water should be incorporated into the framework of integrated and sustainable planning and management of all water resources. To this end, basin-scale planning should establish the objectives and destinations of reused flows, taking into account all available uses and resources, in order to avoid generating expectations in terms of demand and to guarantee ecological flows.

In short, it is essential to apply both efficiency criteria (water savings per unit of unit product or service generated) and effectiveness criteria (reduction of total gross abstraction of water from natural systems, such as rivers and aquifers).

The Cotec Foundation proposes the following set of indicators for measuring "circularity" in the water sector:

- Share of treated water reused (%).
- Share of agricultural demand satisfied by reused water (%).
- Share of urban and industrial non-potable uses covered by reused water (%).
- Share of losses in water distribution networks (%).
- The volume of wastewater incorporating material recovery processes (%).
- Net energy consumption per unit of reused water (KW/m$^3$).
- Share of citizens supporting wastewater reuse (%).

Source: Cotec Foundation (2017[15]), *The Situation and Development of the Circular Economy in Spain*; Spain's Official State Gazette (2007[44]), *Royal Decree 1620/2007 of 7 December 2007 Establishing the Legal Regime for the Reuse of Treated Water*; Iglesias, A., T. Estrela and F. Gallart (2005[43]), "Impactos sobre los recursos hídricos", *Evaluación Preliminar de los Impactos en España for Efecto del Cambio Climático*.

### Urban mobility

Promoting sustainable mobility is amongst the city's objectives and can be further implemented through circular economy approaches, based on material and resource efficiency. The Integrated Sustainable Urban Development Strategy Granada 2014-20 and the Strategy Granada 2020, Making the Urban Human (EG 2020) document the challenges that the city faces in terms of urban mobility. The city faces morphological challenges due to small streets and pronounced slopes in the historical centre. Moreover, intense fluxes of people enter Granada every day from neighbouring municipalities for work. Around 400 000 daily trips originate in Granada's metropolitan area and have the city as the final destination (Granada City Council, 2013[45]). Transport is the largest source of energy consumption, accounting for more than 60% of total consumption and 51% of the city's $CO_2$ emissions (Granada City Council, 2020[9]). Some actions undertaken by the city are the following:

- Promotion of shared mobility schemes: The municipality reduces 50% of the tax on economic activity (*Impuesto a la Actividad Económica*) for those companies that presents a plan to promote shared mobility among their employers (e.g. the beer company Alhambra is offering benefits to employees sharing their cars with other co-workers).
- Increasing infrastructure supply to reduce traffic: In 2017, the city opened the "Metropolitano of Granada" light rail line, with a single line crossing the city from north to south and also connecting with the surrounding municipalities of Albolote, Armilla and Maracena. In addition to reducing commuting time for citizens, the Metropolitano should help avoid the circulation of nearly 8 000 vehicles per day, which would result in an annual saving of 3 232 tonnes of $CO_2$ emissions (Government of Andalusia/Granada City Council, 2020[46]).
- Air quality plan: The municipality of Granada promoted a declaration to improve air quality in the metropolitan area. A total of 23 municipalities committed to approving air quality plans in their

jurisdictions and called for the autonomous government of Andalusia to elaborate its own regional air quality plan.

Circular urban mobility in cities is based on the effective adaptation of people's mobility needs using different means of transport, which impacts quality of life, local environment and consumption of resources. The main advantages of circular mobility are the reduction of: the consumption of virgin materials linked to the transport sector as, thanks to the increased efficiency of infrastructure and mobility, less infrastructure needs to be built to supply the same number of users; waste and pollution; the use of infrastructures (e.g. roads) and vehicles; and operating costs (Ellen MacArthur Foundation, 2019[47]).

Land use and urban mobility have a key role in the building of more sustainable cities and this is also the case for Granada. Transport is one of the sectors with the highest impact in terms of carbon emissions and energy consumption, and there are many opportunities for Granada to design urban mobility structures based on more renewable energies and with lower emissions. This would be particularly beneficial to tackle the city's poor air quality standard. For instance, Granada could focus on shared municipal fleets of cars and bicycles, as well as on developing urban logistic spaces, increasing the attractiveness of the use of public transport, widening sustainable transportation options and building additional bicycle lanes.

*Tourism*

The tourism sector in the city of Granada, with more than 1 700 000 visitors per year, provides an opportunity for job creation and holds potential for applying circular economy principles. The tourism industry is a vast and complex one, covering a variety of sectors and connecting with multiple other industries and value chains – from agriculture to food, to the built environment and transport. Tourism also entails negative effects on the environment, such as high resource consumption and waste production, for example, due to the high energy demand of air conditioning and the deterioration of natural heritage. As such, in Granada, the city and stakeholders have implemented initiatives to reduce the negative environmental impacts of tourism, namely, the Green Footprint project and the Provincial Plan for Adaptation to Climate Change (Box 2.6). However, these initiatives consider circular economy approaches in silos rather than based on collaborations across value chains and stakeholders. Other planning tools focus on competitiveness and quality services, such as the Andalusian Major Cities Tourism Plan for the city of Granada, approved in 2020.

---

**Box 2.6. Initiatives for a sustainable tourism sector in the province of Granada, Spain**

In 2019, the Provincial Federation of Hospitality and Tourism Companies of Granada (La Huella Verde Granada) launched the Green Footprint project (*La Huella Verde*) to: i) educate and raise awareness in the tourism sector in Granada about the degradation of the environment; ii) engage with the private sector to operate on the basis of energy efficiency, good practices and the principles of the circular economy; and iii) transform the city and the province with a view to well-being and quality of life.

The Provincial Plan for Adaptation to Climate Change in Granada (Adapta Granada), launched in 2019, proposes five specific actions which seek to promote tourism models based on sustainable resources and the sustainable seasonally adjustment of the sector: i) creation of greenways and natural itineraries for tourism use; ii) measures to promote tourism based on the territory's resources and with an environmental commitment; iii) seasonal adjustment of tourism activity on the coast; iv) adaptation of municipal budgets to cater for longer summer seasons; and v) adaptation of municipalities to improve the comfort of tourists in the face of heat waves.

Source: La Huella Verde Granada (2019[48]), Homepage, https://www.lahuellaverdegranada.org/ (accessed on 8 January 2021); Provincial Council of Granada (2019[49]), *Climate Change Adaptation Plan*, https://www.dipgra.es/contenidos/plan-adaptacion-al-cambio-climatico/ (accessed on 15 January 2021).

---

Promoting circularity in tourism notably requires incorporating circularity principles in accommodation and food services, through new forms of collaboration and partnerships along the value chain. For example, hotels and other types of accommodation services can: contract rental services (e.g. for specific types of furniture and laundry); implement joint procurement and bundling of waste streams for useful applications; use reusable items and refurbish with recycled materials, wherever possible. An example of this type of collaboration is provided by the Circular Hotels Leaders Group (*Kloplopergroep*) launched in the city of Amsterdam, the Netherlands, in 2018. Regarding food services in restaurants, the first step is to prevent food waste (e.g. replacing buffet with a la carte schemes). Food that is set to go to waste can be sold at a low price on platforms (e.g. Too Good To Go) or donated to food banks. In the longer term, food service managers can seek to foster and support local food production chains, minimising the environmental impact of food production and transport and favouring the longer conservation of raw materials. London in the United Kingdom created the Sustainable Food Places, supporting public authorities and private companies that procure catering contracts promoting the food waste hierarchy, strengthening policies for dedicated space for food waste (and all other recyclables) in all new housing developments. There is currently no food waste legislation in place in Spain. However, the Spanish government announced in 2020 that a new law on food waste (*Ley sobre las Pérdidas y el Desperdicio Alimentario*) will be released in 2021, in line with SDG 12.3 on reduction of global food waste (Government of Spain, 2020[50]).

The COVID-19 pandemic, which stopped travel and tourism, also represents an opportunity to reflect on more sustainable business models for the tourism and hospitality sector. Tourism is the third-largest socio-economic activity in the EU, accounting for 21% of people employed within the services sector. However, since the beginning of the COVID-19 pandemic, the global travel and tourism industry is facing unprecedented economic and existential challenges. Several long-term socio-economic trends will affect the industry in the years to come on both the supply and demand sides (e.g. increasing demand for clear and strict hygiene measures, the pursuit of healthier and more sustainable lifestyles, etc.). To build back better, a new framing of tourism activities is needed, which represents an opportunity for circular economy business models to thrive. Examples of initiatives supporting the green transition and sustainable tourism development as part of the COVID-19 responses include: Corsica, France, which is implementing a roadmap for tourism sustainability; the city of Posio, Finland, which is promoting and investing in sustainability to restore demand; and the Kyoto Destination Management Organisation in Japan, repositioning its recovery strategy to reorient toward local needs and support sustainable growth (OECD, 2020[51]).

## The built environment

Granada can further explore opportunities to apply circular economy principles to the built environment sector. In 2020, Granada joined the European network URGE – Circular Building Cities of the EC URBACT III Action Planning Networks programme, to design, together with eight other European cities,[5] a common strategy aimed at establishing a circular economy system in the built environment sector. Circular practices in the construction sector consist of building using recyclable construction materials, designing buildings that can enhance water and energy efficiency and respond to population shrinking in the city through modular construction and circular building. Examples are reported in Box 2.7.

The national legal framework encourages sustainable water management of buildings during the construction phase. However, there is room for improvement in terms of material management. In Spain, Royal Decree 105/2008 regulates the production and management of construction and demolition waste. Every construction project must include a waste management study, including an estimate of the quantity of construction and demolition waste that would be generated onsite; the measures adopted to prevent waste generation; and the reuse, recovery or disposal operations to be applied for the generated waste during the work (Spain's Official State Gazette, 2008[52]). Designers and constructors can take this practice to the next level and go beyond waste management and focus on material management. The Cluster for Sustainable Construction of Andalusia (CSA) created by the Provincial Council of Granada in 2014 can support this endeavour through collaboration across stakeholders from the private sector (e.g. architects, engineers, developers, builders, installers, material manufacturers, window manufacturers, photovoltaic panel manufacturers), sectoral and educational institutions, including the University of Granada (CSA, 2021[29]).

---

### Box 2.7. Circular economy principles applied to the built environment

The circular way of building consists of rethinking upstream and downstream processes to minimise waste production and maximise resource use. It also implies new forms of collaborations amongst designers, constructors, contractors, real estate investors, suppliers of low- and high-tech building materials and owners, while looking at the life cycle from construction to end of life. According to the OECD (2020[13]), there are some key phases to stimulate circular building: planning, design, construction, operation and end of current life.

- **Planning** in a circular manner means considering the entire life cycle of the asset, including alternative use through repurposing and reassembly. Examples are modular approaches so that materials and building blocks can be easily dismantled and reused. The city of Amsterdam, the Netherlands, applies smart design for buildings more suitable for the repurposing and reuse of materials and improves efficiency in the dismantling and separation of waste streams to enable high-value reuse and to create a resource bank and marketplace where materials can be exchanged between market players.

- **Design** in the project phase takes into account the material choice, the consumption of water and energy in buildings to reduce consumption and minimise waste and possible reuse of buildings. In Belgium, the Public Waste Agency of Flanders (OVAM) in collaboration with the Walloon Public Service (SPW) and environment agency Brussels Environment developed an online open-access calculation tool called Tool to Optimise the Total Environmental Impact of Materials (TOTEM). TOTEM helps architects, designers and builders to assess the environmental impact of building materials to increase the material and energy performance of buildings.

- The **choice of materials for the construction** phase entails identifying more sustainable materials and minimising the variety of materials used. The use of certifications to ensure the minimum circular standards, material passports and material banks can foster reuse of construction materials and provide constructors and clients with reused materials. In the city of Paris, France, besides meeting all mandatory requirements established in the NF Habitat HQE Base standards, a certification for the building sector, construction projects must reach at least 40% of the points established in a "circular economy profile" to be considered circular (e.g. inclusion of a waste management plan, use of recycled materials, development of life-analysis calculations, eco-certification of wood, considering deconstruction processes, establishing synergies with local actors in the surrounding areas, among others).

- The **operation** phase concerns the use of energy sources and embedded technologies in buildings to enhance resource efficiency. The operation also includes the use of data and innovative technologies as enablers to extending the life assets, which delay the shift towards a second life or end of life. For example, the city of Paris recovers heat from wastewater to heat and cool public buildings and has also developed a network of non-potable water users to optimise water consumption. Maribor, Slovenia, has deployed a spatial analysis of the use and production of heat in the city to optimise energy use.

- The **end life** of a building could create a new life for the waste material produced. Three levels of circularity can be identified: repurposing an existing asset, components and materials with no major transformations and in the same location; reusing an existing asset for the same purpose but in a different location; reusing components and materials of existing assets, in the same and different location. Particular attention is paid to spatial planning, given the city's relatively strong role as commissioning authority for public spaces and in the realisation of its own accommodation and granting of permits for construction and demolition.

Source: OECD (2020[13]), *The Circular Economy in Cities and Regions: Synthesis Report*, https://doi.org/10.1787/10ac6ae4-en.

### *Places*

The circular economy can be applied at various scales, from the neighbourhood to the regional level and create linkages across urban and rural areas. In Granada, further links can be exploited between the urban core and the surrounding rural area home of agricultural production, accounting for 8.6% of total employment in the province in 2018, double the level in Spain (4.2%) (Unicaja, 2020[53]). The pact to protect the Vega of Granada, an agricultural and livestock farming area comprising 41 municipalities including the city of Granada, foresees the adoption of 10 principles, from updating land use norms to protecting agricultural land and promoting local food production (Pacto por la Vega de Granada, 2015[54]).

One of the fields with potential for improvement in the city of Granada and the province is the search for solutions for the reuse of agro-food waste. There are examples of companies at the national level that are promoting the conversion of agri-food waste into raw materials and powdered ingredients (AgroSingularity, 2021[55]). This system would allow farmers to market their by-products while generating environmental, social and economic benefits (Box 2.8).

Local food can be used in hospitals, schools and universities as a way to reduce transport costs and related GHG emissions and to minimise the risk of shortages in case of shock or blocked transport. Many cities have implemented systems to promote local food. For example, the city of Paris is planning to relocate part of its food production to reduce transport costs and related GHG emissions. In Maribor, Slovenia, a digital platform (INNO RURAL) connects local food producers and customers to shorten delivery routes and share information on the type of products that are sold and where they are sold (OECD, 2020[13]).

### Box 2.8. Spanish regulatory framework for by-products

Directive 2008/98/EC on waste and its transposition to the Spanish state through Law 22/2011 on waste and contaminated soils defines the conditions for a substance or object, resulting from a production process and whose purpose is not the production of that substance or object, to be considered as a by-product and not as waste, when the following conditions are met:

- There is a certainty that the substance or object will be used at a later date.
- The substance or object can be used directly without further processing except by common industrial practice.
- The substance or object is produced as an integral part of a production process.
- Further use meets all relevant requirements relating to products and the protection of human health and the environment.

In order to consider a substance or object as a by-product, these four conditions must be fulfilled simultaneously. Otherwise, it will be classified as waste.

The process to regulate the declaration of production waste as a by-product is sequenced in two main phases. First, for the general application for a by-product declaration, the Working Group of the Waste

Coordination Committee of the Ministry for the Ecological Transition and the Demographic Challenge of Spain assesses the compliance with the conditions for the specific use of the production waste concerned. In the second phase, the intention to use the relevant production waste as a by-product needs to be notified to the autonomous community where the production waste is generated, as well as to the autonomous community of destination.

In June 2020, the Spanish government initiated the public information process for the draft bill on waste and contaminated soil, repealing Law 22/2011. The draft bill determines when waste can be reused and establishes two categories: waste that is in fact a resource for remanufacturing the same product; or a by-product, a secondary product derived from industrial processes.

One of the main modifications of the draft bill is the obligation to keep a chronological register of the entities or companies that generate by-products and those that use them. The text empowers the autonomous communities to implement it in their territories, which is expected to facilitate the existence of a market or demand for such substances or objects.

Source: Government of Spain (2021[56]), *Working Group on By-products and End-of-Waste Status*, https://www.miteco.gob.es/es/calidad-y-evaluacion-ambiental/temas/prevencion-y-gestion-residuos/comision-coordinacion/Procedimiento-Evaluacion-Subproducto.aspx; Government of Spain (2017[57]), *By-product Evaluation Procedure*.

## References

AgroSingularity (2021), *Homepage*, http://www.agrosingularity.com/ (accessed on 1 February 2021).  [55]

Barcelona City Council (2021), *Barcelona Superblock: New Stage*, https://ajuntament.barcelona.cat/superilles/en/ (accessed on 7 April 2021).  [24]

Barcelona Urban Ecology Agency (2021), *Superblocks*, http://www.bcnecologia.net/es/modelo-conceptual/supermanzana (accessed on 3 February 2021).  [23]

Congress of Deputies (2021), *Spanish Draft Law on Climate Change and Energy Transition*, https://www.congreso.es/backoffice_doc/prensa/notas_prensa/81345_1617867418184.pdf.  [2]

Cotec Foundation (2017), *The Situation and Development of the Circular Economy in Spain*.  [15]

Covenant of Mayors (2020), *Granada*, http://www.pactodelosalcaldes.eu (accessed on 1 April 2021).  [10]

CSA (2021), *Quiénes Somos*, Cluster CSA, https://clustercsa.com/quienes-somos/ (accessed on 15 January 2021).  [29]

Debates de Granada (2018), "«Re-visiones» urbanas. Nuevos fundamentos de la actividad urbanística en España, conferencias y mesa de debate en la E.T.S. de Arquitectura", https://canal.ugr.es/noticia/re-visiones-urbanas-conferencias-debate-arquitectura/ (accessed on 10 February 2021).  [20]

Ecoembes (2015), "Consumidores comprometidos con el reciclaje", https://www.ecoembes.com/es/planeta-recicla/blog/consumidores-comprometidos-con-el-reciclaje (accessed on 21 January 2021).  [31]

Ellen MacArthur Foundation (2019), *Circular Economies in Cities*, [47]
http://www.ellenmacarthurfoundation.org/our-work/activities/circular-economy-in-cities
(accessed on 7 April 2021).

European Union (2019), *Report on Sustainable Finance for a Circular Economy*, Publications [38]
Office of the European Union, http://dx.doi.org/10.2779/171661.

Government of Andalusia (2020), *Draft Bill for the Circular Economy Law of Andalusia*, [5]
https://www.juntadeandalucia.es/boja/2020/235/36 (accessed on 22 January 2021).

Government of Andalusia (2019), *Acuerdo de formulación del Plan Integral de Residuos de* [4]
*Andalucía. Hacia una Economía Circular en el Horizonte 2030 (PIRec 2030)*,
http://www.juntadeandalucia.es/eboja (accessed on 11 January 2021).

Government of Andalusia (2018), *Andalusian Strategy for the Circular Bioeconomy*, [6]
https://www.juntadeandalucia.es/organismos/sobre-junta/planes/detalle/155202.html
(accessed on 5 April 2021).

Government of Andalusia (2018), *Estrategia Andaluza de Desarrollo Sostenible 2030*, [3]
https://eco-circular.com/wp-content/uploads/2018/06/edas_2030.pdf (accessed on
11 January 2021).

Government of Andalusia/Granada City Council (2020), *Plan Turístico de Grandes Ciudades de* [46]
*Andalucía de la ciudad de Granada*,
https://www.juntadeandalucia.es/organismos/turismoregeneracionjusticiayadministracionlocal
/consejeria/sobre-consejeria/planes/detalle/206317.html (accessed on 15 January 2021).

Government of Spain (2021), *Working Group on By-products and End-of-Waste Status*, [56]
https://www.miteco.gob.es/es/calidad-y-evaluacion-ambiental/temas/prevencion-y-gestion-
residuos/comision-coordinacion/Procedimiento-Evaluacion-Subproducto.aspx (accessed on
27 January 2021).

Government of Spain (2020), *España Circular 2030, Estrategia Española de Economía Circular*. [1]

Government of Spain (2020), "Planas: El acuerdo para la nueva PAC es un buen punto de [50]
partida para responder a las necesidades del sector agrario",
https://www.lamoncloa.gob.es/serviciosdeprensa/notasprensa/agricultura/Paginas/2020/1211
20-pac.aspx (accessed on 14 January 2021).

Government of Spain (2017), *By-product Evaluation Procedure*. [57]

Granada City Council (2021), *Cleaning and Waste Collection*, [34]
https://www.granada.org/inet/wambiente.nsf/xresiduos (accessed on 26 January 2021).

Granada City Council (2021), *Memoria Justificativa de la elección de la gestión indirecta del* [35]
*servicio de limpieza viaria y recogida de residuos*.

Granada City Council (2021), *Waste Collection Data*, [33]
https://www.granada.org/inet/wambiente.nsf/wwtod/811B713743BE80E4C12583C90040758
E (accessed on 26 January 2021).

**56** |

Granada City Council (2020), *Circular Economy and Recycling: The Solution for the Environment*, https://www.granada.org/inet/educa.nsf/a665e4813cfe0314c1257999003beee3/a36e14e2a97 0d572c125845e00256b2e!OpenDocument (accessed on 26 January 2021). [11]

Granada City Council (2020), *Estrategia de Desarrollo Urbano Sostenible e Integrado de Granada 2014-2020*. [9]

Granada City Council (2020), *Medio Ambiente*, https://www.granada.org/inet/wambiente.nsf (accessed on 7 April 2021). [36]

Granada City Council (2019), "El Ayuntamiento elabora un Plan de Actuación que sitúa Granada a la vanguardia de la prevención del riesgo de inundaciones", https://www.granada.org/inet/wprensa.nsf/9c3fdb2a0697eae5c1256ec500376c62/4c58d53ad d421adbc125849b0042ea5c!OpenDocument (accessed on 7 April 2021). [41]

Granada City Council (2019), *Ordenanza fiscal nº 25 reguladora de la tasa por recogida de residuos municipales y tratamiento de residuos sólidos municipales*, https://www.granada.org/inet/wgr.nsf/a126af4ba2d43677c1256dfe002c51b8/b9e2a01fd0875d a0c12584fc003c52ac!OpenDocument (accessed on 2 February 2021). [37]

Granada City Council (2013), *Plan de Movilidad Urbana Sostenible de Granada*. [45]

Granada Ciudad de la Ciencia y la Innovación (2019), "Charlas en lugares singulares: Investigación en Alimentación «made in Granada»", http://www.granadaciencia.es/actividades/charlas-en-lugares-singulares-investigacion-en-alimentacion-made-in-granada/ (accessed on 11 January 2021). [28]

Granada Hoy (2020), "El gran contrato de la limpieza de Granada, en cifras", https://www.granadahoy.com/granada/gran-contrato-limpieza-Granada-cifras_0_1522348124.html (accessed on 8 January 2021). [58]

Hidralia (2021), "Hidralia, hacia la neutralidad en carbono y la eficiencia energética", http://www.hidralia-sa.es/-/hidralia-hacia-la-neutralidad-en-carbono-y-la-eficiencia-energetica (accessed on 8 February 2021). [39]

Iglesias, A., T. Estrela and F. Gallart (2005), "Impactos sobre los recursos hídricos", *Evaluación Preliminar de los Impactos en España for Efecto del Cambio Climático*. [43]

Inagra (2020), *Servicio de muebles solidarios*, https://www.inagra.es/muebles-solidarios/# (accessed on 30 March 2021). [12]

IUC (2020), *Smart Cities and Blockchain Innovations - IUC Pilot Project Granada Competitive Fund - Webinar 1*, International Urban Cooperation, https://www.iuc-asia.eu/2020/10/smart-cities-and-blockchain-innovations-iuc-pilot-project-granada-competitive-fund-webinar-1/ (accessed on 25 January 2021). [26]

La Huella Verde Granada (2021), *Acreditación Medioambiental*, Confederation of Tourism and Hospitality of Granada, http://www.lahuellaverdegranada.org/acreditacion-medioambiental/ (accessed on 1 February 2021). [30]

La Huella Verde Granada (2019), *Homepage*, Provincial Federation of Hospitality and Tourism Companies of Granada, https://www.lahuellaverdegranada.org/ (accessed on 8 January 2021). [48]

Mueller, N. et al. (2020), "Changing the urban design of cities for health: The superblock model", *Environment International*, Vol. 134, p. 105132, http://dx.doi.org/10.1016/j.envint.2019.105132. [25]

OECD (2020), "Mitigating the impact of COVID-19 on tourism and supporting recovery", *OECD Tourism Papers*, No. 2020/03, OECD Publishing, Paris, https://dx.doi.org/10.1787/47045bae-en. [51]

OECD (2020), *The Circular Economy in Cities and Regions: Synthesis Report*, OECD Urban Studies, OECD Publishing, Paris, https://dx.doi.org/10.1787/10ac6ae4-en. [13]

OECD (2019), *OECD Principles on Urban Policy*, OECD, Paris. [32]

OECD (2016), *Water Governance in Cities*, OECD Studies on Water, OECD Publishing, Paris, https://dx.doi.org/10.1787/9789264251090-en. [14]

Pacto por la Vega de Granada (2015), *Pacto por la Vega de Granada*, http://salvemoslavega.org/wp-content/uploads/2020/12/Pacto-por-la-Vega-de-Granada.pdf (accessed on 11 January 2021). [54]

Provincial Council of Granada (2020), "Diputación acoge unas jornadas virtuales sobre economía circular en las que da a conocer experiencias de la provincia", http://www.dipgra.es/amplia-actualidad/noticias-inicio/diputacion-acoge-unas-jornadas-virtuales-economia-circular-que-da-conocer-experiencias-provincia (accessed on 15 January 2021). [7]

Provincial Council of Granada (2019), *Climate Change Adaptation Plan*, https://www.dipgra.es/contenidos/plan-adaptacion-al-cambio-climatico/ (accessed on 15 January 2021). [49]

Provincial Council of Granada (2014), *Municipal Waste Management Programme for the Province of Granada 2014-2024*, http://www.resurgranada.es/descargas_publicas.php (accessed on 25 January 2021). [8]

PTS Granada (2021), *Homepage*, Parque Tecnológico de la Salud, https://ptsgranada.com/ (accessed on 26 January 2021). [27]

Sahuquillo Herráiz, A. (2009), "La importancia de las aguas subterraneas (coste/uso intensivo/almacenamiento subterráneo/uso conjunto/protección acuíferos)", *Revista de la Real Academia de Ciencias Exactas, Fisicas y Naturales*, pp. 97-114. [42]

Spain's Official State Gazette (2007), *Royal Decree 1620/2007 of 7 December 2007 Establishing the Legal Regime for the Reuse of Treated Water*. [44]

Spain's Official State Gazette (2008), *Real Decreto 105/2008, de 1 de febrero, por el que se regula la producción y gestión de los residuos de construcción y demolición*, https://www.boe.es/buscar/pdf/2008/BOE-A-2008-2486-consolidado.pdf (accessed on 11 January 2021). [52]

Spanish Environment Congress (2016), "La supermanzana viaja desde Vitoria y Barcelona hasta Nueva York", http://www.conama2016.org/web/es/prensa/noticias/la-supermanzana-viaja-desde-vitoria-y-barcelona-hasta-nueva-york.html (accessed on 6 November 2019). [22]

Transecto (2020), "Parques inundables: el rol del espacio público en la gestión del agua", https://transecto.com/2020/05/parques-inundables/ (accessed on 7 April 2021). [40]

UGR (2020), "Debates "ODS: Una llamada a la acción": ¿Para qué sirve la Economía Circular? Una realidad formativa en la Universidad de Granada", https://canal.ugr.es/evento/debates-ods-una-llamada-a-la-accion-para-que-sirve-la-economia-circular-una-realidad-formativa-en-la-universidad-de-granada/ (accessed on 30 March 2021). [19]

UGR (2020), "La UGR apuesta por la economía circular inclusiva con la instalación de puntos limpios en sus instalaciones", https://canal.ugr.es/noticia/la-ugr-apuesta-por-la-economia-circular-inclusiva-con-la-instalacion-de-puntos-limpios-en-sus-instalaciones/ (accessed on 30 March 2021). [18]

Unicaja (2020), *Informe Anual del Sector Agrario en Andalucia 2018*, http://www.analistaseconomicos.com (accessed on 31 March 2021). [53]

University of Granada (2019), "Introducción a la economía circular y a la estrategia del plástico", https://fciencias.ugr.es/34-noticias/3198-introduccion-a-la-economia-circular-y-a-la-estrategia-del-plastico (accessed on 2 February 2021). [17]

University of Granada (2019), *Tecnologías para la economía circular*, https://tep968.ugr.es/datos_inicio/lineas_investigacion/ (accessed on 11 January 2021). [16]

University of Granada (2018), "La UGR firma un conjunto de convenios que contribuyen a fortalecer el tejido productivo de Granada", https://canal.ugr.es/noticia/ugr-convenios-programa-granada-colabora-inncuba/ (accessed on 11 January 2021). [21]

## Notes

[1] A number of regional ministries of Andalusia and institutions contributed to the strategy, such as: the Regional Ministry of Economy and Knowledge (*Consejería de Economía y Conocimiento*); the Andalusian Knowledge Agency (*Agencia Andaluza del Conocimiento*); the Institute of Statistics and Cartography of Andalusia (*Instituto Estadística y Cartografía de Andalucía*); the Regional Ministry of Employment, Enterprise and Trade (*Consejería de Empleo, Empresa y Comercio*); the Andalusian Energy Agency (*Agencia Andaluza de la Energía*); the Innovation and Development Agency of Andalusia (*Agencia de Innovación y Desarrollo de Andalucía*); the Regional Ministry for Environment and Territorial Planning (*Consejería de Media Ambiente y Ordenación del Territorio*); the Andalusian Institute of Agricultural and Fisheries Research and Training (*Instituto de Investigación y Formación Agraria y Pesquera*); the Andalusian Agricultural and Fisheries Management Agency (*Agencia de Gestión Agraria y Pesquera de Andalucía*); the Regional Ministry of Agriculture, Fisheries and Rural Development (*Consejería de Agricultura, Pesca y Desarrollo Rural*).

[2] The Delegation of Employment and Sustainable Development of the Granada Provincial Council is participating in the Color Circle project on the circular economy, committing to inter-regional co-operation with European partners from the Czech Republic, France, the Netherlands and Romania. The aim is to empower local entities, connecting them with research teams, towards the full development of the circular

economy. This action is carried out within the framework of the European programme Interreg Europe, financed by the European Regional Development Fund (ERDF).

[1] See http://www.bcnecologia.net/es/modelo-conceptual/supermanzana.

[2] See https://ec.europa.eu/environment/europeangreencapital/winning-cities/2012-vitoria-gasteiz/.

[3] The IUC is an EU Foreign Policy Instrument (FPI) programme that boosts international urban co-operation with EU partners in Asia and the Americas.

[4] Emasagra issues bimonthly receipts for the waste collection charge to every household, whether or not they receive the water service.

[5] The participating cities are: Copenhagen (Denmark), Intermunicipal Community of the West (Portugal), Kavala (Greece), Munich (Germany), Nigrad (Slovenia), Prato (Italy), Riga (Latvia) and Utrecht (Netherlands).

# 3 Governance challenges to the circular transition

This chapter describes the main challenges that Granada is facing in the transition from a linear to a circular economy. The analysis focuses on five main categories of gaps: policy, awareness, capacity, regulatory and funding. Major issues highlighted in the chapter are related to the weak vertical and horizontal co-ordination, which can inhibit a holistic approach to the circular economy, the need to raise awareness of the circular economy as well as to build capacities across public bodies and the business sector.

## Governance gaps in the circular economy in cities

Building on the OECD framework "Mind the Gaps: Bridge the Gaps" (Charbit and Michalun, 2009[1]) and the OECD report on Water Governance in OECD countries (2011[2]), the OECD report *The Circular Economy in Cities and Regions* (OECD, 2020[3]) identified five types of governance gaps cities face when designing and implementing a circular economy (Figure 3.1). In particular, 51 surveyed cities and regions highlighted the following gaps:

- *Funding gap*: Cities and regions face constraints in terms of insufficient financial resources (73%), financial risks (69%), lack of critical scale for business and investments (59%) and lack of private sector engagement (43%).

- *Regulatory gap*: Inadequate regulatory framework and incoherent regulation across levels of government represent a challenge for respectively 73% and 55% of surveyed cities and regions.

- *Policy gap*: A lack of holistic vision is an obstacle for surveyed cities and regions (67%). This can be due to poor leadership and co-ordination. Other policy gaps concern the lack of political will.

- *Awareness gap*: Cultural barriers represent a challenge for 67% of surveyed cities and regions along with a lack of awareness (63%) and inadequate information (55%) for policymakers to take decisions, businesses to innovate and residents to embrace sustainable consumption patterns.

- *Capacity gap*: The lack of human resources is a challenge for 61% of surveyed cities and regions. Technical capacities should not just aim for optimising linear systems but strive towards changing relations across value chains and preventing resource waste.

### Figure 3.1. Main obstacles to the circular economy in 51 cities and regions

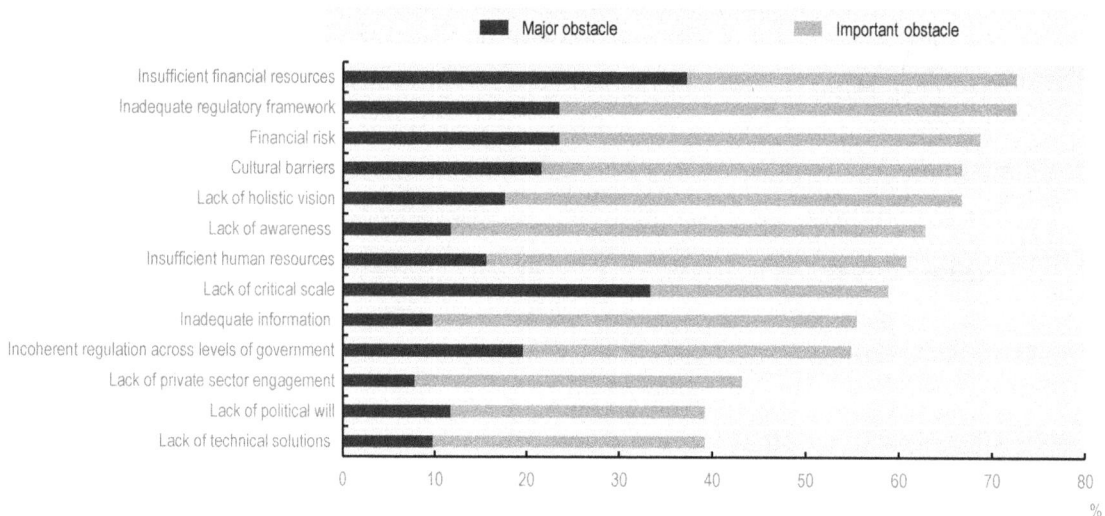

Note: Results based on a sample of 51 respondents that indicated obstacles as being "Major" and "Important".
Source: OECD (2020[3]), *The Circular Economy in Cities and Regions: Synthesis Report*, https://doi.org/10.1787/10ac6ae4-en.

## Governance gaps in Granada, Spain

In Granada, key governance challenges relate to: weak co-ordination among municipal departments and across levels of government, which may hinder policy coherence; the lack of awareness of policymakers, businesses and citizens on what circular economy entails; the lack of technical and human resources at the municipal level for linking existing strategies to a circular economy vision; the lack of economic instruments to incentivise sustainable behaviours; and the lack of circular economy principles in public procurement. Figure 3.2 provide a summary of the gaps, identified through ad hoc interviews with more than 70 stakeholders in the city.

## Figure 3.2. Governance gaps for a circular economy in Granada

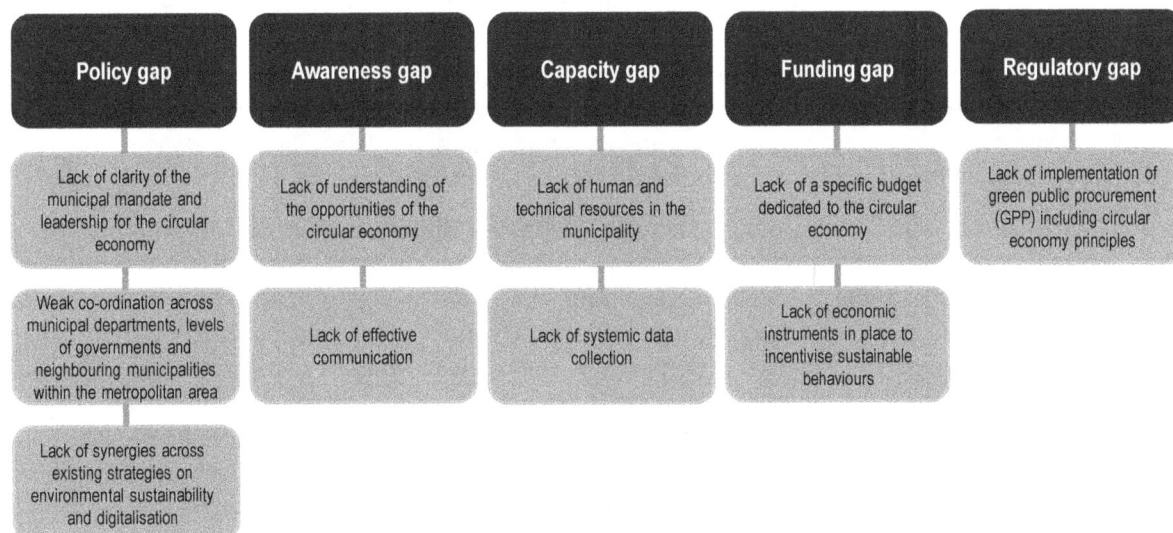

| Policy gap | Awareness gap | Capacity gap | Funding gap | Regulatory gap |
|---|---|---|---|---|
| Lack of clarity of the municipal mandate and leadership for the circular economy | Lack of understanding of the opportunities of the circular economy | Lack of human and technical resources in the municipality | Lack of a specific budget dedicated to the circular economy | Lack of implementation of green public procurement (GPP) including circular economy principles |
| Weak co-ordination across municipal departments, levels of governments and neighbouring municipalities within the metropolitan area | Lack of effective communication | Lack of systemic data collection | Lack of economic instruments in place to incentivise sustainable behaviours | |
| Lack of synergies across existing strategies on environmental sustainability and digitalisation | | | | |

### Policy gap

Policy gaps relate to the lack of leadership, co-ordination across municipal departments and levels of government, which in turn undermine policy coherence. As the circular economy is systemic by nature, a cross-sectoral approach is needed to ensure that the city rethinks urban policies and their relation with resource efficiency holistically, beyond the optimisation of the existing policies towards the achievement of targeted environmental goals, such as $CO_2$ emission reduction.

The mandate in terms of who is the lead institution for the design and implementation of a circular economy strategy in the city administration is yet to be defined. The development of a circular vision in Granada requires a clarification of the role of the municipality in the design and implementation of a circular economy vision, as well as a definition of the roles and responsibilities of the different municipal departments. On the one hand, while Emasagra, the public-private water utility company, initiates a reflection on the transition to the circular economy in the city through the circular biofactory (Granada Sur Biorefinery), the municipality is responsible for raising the profile of the circular economy in the city council's agenda. So far, the departments that have been mostly involved in the dialogue with Emasagra on the circular economy or that are debating on how to transition towards the circular economy in the future, are those linked to public works and urban development, the economy, public-private companies, treasury and innovation and the environment. Strong leadership to accelerate the circular economy transition and horizontal coordination will be needed.

Municipal departments need to strengthen co-ordination to maximise synergies and investments for the circular economy. At present, there are neither incentives for horizontal co-ordination at the technical level, nor specific co-ordination mechanisms or joint programmes across municipal departments. For example, there is little connection between the urban planning and mobility departments (e.g. regarding the functions of managing and planning transport lines or measures aiming to reduce car use in the city that require co-ordinating public transportation policies with the use of parking lots and future car-sharing options). However, aligning these areas is crucial to develop sustainable and integrated urban development plans in a more circular way, for example, to change how city districts are designed, without necessarily creating additional infrastructure (e.g. by allocating existing parking lots for car-sharing and bicycles instead of private vehicles).

Policy coherence should be fostered in Granada. Recently, the city set up policies and plans to enhance environmental sustainability and digitalisation, such as the Strategy for Sustainable and Integrated Urban Development of Granada (EDUSI) and Granada's Smart City Strategic Plan 2020. However, it is not clear how they are connected and how they would benefit from a certain level of co-ordination, in terms of investments, human and technical resources. Similarly, the Emasagra biofactory through which the overall debate about implementing a circular economy in the city started, could be better connected with the urban fabric. For instance, the compost produced is reused in agricultural activities but there does not seem to be an explicit link with local food production injected into an urban food strategy.

More effective co-ordination across neighbouring municipalities within the metropolitan area is needed. Within the metropolitan area, neighbouring municipalities hold responsibility for joint actions on public transport services, drinking water supply services and maintenance of the sewerage and wastewater treatment network, among others. However, each municipality makes individual decisions without a joint vision or plan. For example, in the case of transport, a Metropolitan Transport Consortium is in place to serve the metropolitan area but the city of Granada is not part of it. This implies that the transport policy and its tariff system does not necessarily facilitate multi-modality, which in turn is important given that, every day, 300 000 cars from the metropolitan area commute to the city of Granada for work, while there only 90 000 commute from the capital to the surrounding area (Granada City Council, 2013[4]). Regarding the waste sector, each municipality can hire its own waste collection service, which can hamper co-ordination for joint initiatives and economy of scale, while treatment is carried out within the provincial waste treatment plant located at Alhendin. In the water sector, Aguasvira and Emasagra are the main providers of water services in Granada and its metropolitan area. Aguasvira serves 22 of the 33 municipalities located north of Granada that are part of the Public Consortium for the Development of the Vega-Sierra Elvira (*Consorcio para el Desarrollo de la Vega-Sierra Elvira*). The consortium is responsible for the economic, social and environmental development of its member municipalities and for providing essential public services like water (Vega Sierra Elvira Consortium, 2021[5]).

Co-ordination with the national, regional and provincial governments is also needed to align goals and actions. The province of Granada set up the Municipal Waste Management Programme for the Province of Granada 2014-24; the regional government issued the Andalusian Circular Bioeconomy Strategy, the Strategy for Sustainable Development 2030 and the Andalusian Autonomous Region Integrated Waste Strategy. The national government set the National Circular Economy Strategy (*España Circular 2030*). As such, while initiatives on the circular economy are starting to flourish, further co-ordination would be needed to reach common goals and optimise financial resources. There are networks that can provide room for dialogue across levels of government and municipalities within the province. This is the case of the network of municipalities towards sustainability (Red GRAMAS) bringing together 128 municipalities in the province of Granada. The network carries out its activities through six workgroups focusing on water, energy, waste, urban environment, health, biodiversity, citizen participation and environmental education. However, the municipality of Granada is not part of it. The network's goal is to provide a space where the member municipalities can exchange experiences and design policy solutions that can foster sustainability in their jurisdictions.

### Awareness gap

In Granada, the circular economy is an incipient concept that lacks full understanding from local authorities, the business sector and citizens. The university set up courses on the circular economy and carries out research on related topics, such as water and waste management, eco-friendly construction, sustainable materials, and plastics. However, beyond specific academic environments, there is a generalised lack of understanding of what the circular economy entails. Through the biofactory, the water operator Emasagra is considered the only example of existing circular economy activity in the city. The municipality focuses on green policies especially in regard to sustainable mobility since it represents an important priority for residents' well-being. Still, the large potential concerning closing loops in the touristic and hospitality sector, for example, which represents one of the most important economic sources of the city, is not integrated into local planning. The private sector shows some initiatives in relation to waste recycling, but there are no forms of collaboration across the value chain to close loops.

Communication about opportunities related to the circular economy is lacking. By 2021, the city of Granada will set up a newsletter on the circular economy, which is a first step to raise awareness amongst citizens and engage them in public policymaking and implementation. As agents who can make a real change in the city, they must be empowered. Also, if the city of Granada is to develop a long-term vision of the circular economy, clear communication to the business sector, in terms of how the city is supporting circular economy-related activities, would be needed. A more fluid and structured communication channel across companies, universities and public administration is required to move beyond personal connection. There is room to improve collaboration between the University of Granada, the Granada Health Technology Park and the municipality of Granada as part of the Bureau for Science created by the municipality of Granada to promote dialogue and research on science and innovation.

## *Capacity gap*

The lack of understanding of the opportunities that the circular economy can provide is linked to the lack of human and technical capacities within the municipality. While the city has recently applied to international calls mainly on culture and digitalisation (e.g. European Capital of Culture 2031 and the Digital Transformation Challenge), less attention is given to major "green" initiatives and none on the circular economy. The transition towards the circular economy can be led and supported by a dynamic, competent and motivated team within the municipality.

There is room for systemic data collection that could improve the decision-making process of circular economy-related initiatives. The city has been recently working on developing a data system to incorporate environmental, mobility and energy consumption indicators. However, problems related to implementation are delaying its operability, mainly due to difficulties in reaching a high level of detail of some variables (e.g. noise, air quality level). When available, the platform should be able to show records of noise and air pollution levels, real-time traffic information, among others. Having an adequate information system that would facilitate measuring the progress made could help raise awareness towards more sustainable production and consumption patterns). A harmonised data platform could be used for taking decisions within the circular economy transition. The circular economy strategy in Spain uses an indicator system based on the European monitoring framework for the circular economy (Box 3.1).

### Box 3.1. Measuring the circular economy in Spain

The circular economy strategy in Spain measures progress based on the monitoring framework for the circular economy by the European Commission (EC). Within this framework, the indicators to assess the implementation of the Spanish strategy, mainly based on Eurostat, are as follows:

| Area | Suggested indicators |
|---|---|
| Production and consumption | • Domestic Materials Consumption (Million tonnes) |
| | • Self-sufficiency in the production of critical raw materials in the EU (%) |
| | • Green public procurement (Number, EUR) |
| | • Municipal waste generation per person (kg/inhabitant) |
| | • Waste generation (excluding waste from mineral waste) as a share of gross domestic product (GDP) (kg/EUR) |
| | • Waste generation (excluding waste from mineral waste) relative to household consumption of materials (%) |
| | • Food waste (tonnes) |
| Waste management | • Preparing for reuse (%) |
| | • Municipal waste recycling rate (% (tonnes)) |
| | • Recycling rate of waste excluding mineral waste (% (tonnes)) |
| | • Packaging waste recycling rate (% (tonnes)) |
| | • Plastic packaging waste recycling rate (% (tonnes)) |
| | • Recycling rate of wood packaging waste (% (tonnes)) |
| | • Electric and electronic equipment waste recycling rate (%) |
| | • Organic waste recycling rate (kg/inhabitant) |
| | • Construction and demolition waste recycling rate (NA) |
| Secondary raw materials | • End-of-life product waste recycling rates (%) |
| | • Circular material rate (%) |
| | • Imports from third countries (NA) |
| | • Exports from third countries (NA) |
| | • Intra-EU imports (NA) |
| | • Intra-EU exports (NA) |
| Competitiveness and Innovation | • Gross investment in tangible goods (%) |
| | • Number of jobs (%) |
| | • Value-added at factor cost (%) |
| | • Patents related to recycling and secondary raw materials as a proxy for innovation (Number) |
| Climate change | • Greenhouse gas contribution in the waste sector ($CO_2$ eq (kt)) |

In 2017, the Cotec Foundation, a Spanish organisation to promote innovation, presented the report *The Circular Economy in Spain*, which analyses the state of the art and evaluates the circular transition in the country. The document proposes the following indicators:

| Area | Suggested indicators |
|---|---|
| Input material | • Resource productivity: Relationship between GDP and material consumption (EUR/t) |
| | • Raw materials consumption: Domestic consumption of raw materials (NA) |
| | • Domestic material consumption: Materials used in direct domestic extraction and direct consumption activities in an |

| | economy (Million tonnes) |
|---|---|
| | • National materials requirement: Accumulated mass of primary materials extracted from the natural environment by economic activities (Million tonnes) |
| | • National extraction of materials: Material flows extracted from the territory for further processing or consumption (Million tonnes) |
| Ecodesign | • Life cycle durability: The period of time from the manufacture of a product to its last effective use (Months, years) |
| Production | • Waste generation by sector: Share of waste generated by each productive sector ((Tonnes/total), %) |
| | • By-product exchange: Share of waste generated by each production sector, by-product groups ((Tonnes/total), %) |
| Consumption | • Consumer waste generation: Share of waste generated for each unit of materials consumed ((Tonnes/total), %) |
| Recycling | • Recycling rate by waste category: Percentage of waste recycled ((Tonnes/total), %) |
| Energy | • Energy intensity: Ratio of energy consumption to the volume of economic activity (E/EUR) |
| | • Renewable energy: Share of renewable energy use in total energy mix |
| Climate | • Carbon intensity: Total carbon emissions to GDP (t$CO_2$/EUR) |
| Water | • Reused water resources: Share of water reused (m³, (%)) |
| Land | • Built-up area: Total urbanised area (km²) |
| Food | • Reduction of food waste (NA) |
| Built environment | • Energy efficiency in buildings (NA) |
| Innovation | • Research and development (R&D) in the circular economy (NA) |
| Taxation and pricing | • Tax on waste (NA) |
| | • Tax incentives for by-products (NA) |
| Tourism | • Waste flows generated as a result of tourism (NA) |

Source: Cotec Foundation (2017[6]), *The Circular Economy in Spain*, https://cotec.es/proyecto/informe-economia-circular-en-espana-2017/; Government of Spain (2020[7]), *España Circular 2030, Estrategia Española de Economía Circular*; EC (2018[8]), *Monitoring Framework for the Circular Economy*, https://ec.europa.eu/environment/circular-economy/pdf/monitoring-framework.pdf.

### *Funding gap*

There is neither a specific budget allocated for the transition towards a circular economy, nor specific funds dedicated to the promotion of a circular economy. Following the example of many other cities, Granada could explore opportunities for funding options to enable the transition towards the circular economy. For example, the city of Valladolid, Spain, subsidised 61 projects between 2017 and 2018, related to the circular economy (whether concerning a new design for more durable products, use of secondary materials in production processes or transformation of waste into resources). The grants helped companies start their businesses, although further measures would be needed to scale up the activities and their financial sustainability over time.

There are no economic instruments in place to incentivise sustainable behaviours. For example, the waste fee is not exclusively based on criteria to reduce waste production, since households pay according to the category of street in which they are located, with a total of seven different grades (Granada City Council, 2020[9]). Some cities have put in place discounts, environmental taxes and differentiated tariffs. For instance, with the aim of stimulating the separate disposal of food waste, the city of San Sebastian, Spain, provided households with a specific organic waste bin located in the street and unlockable through a personal magnetic card. The use of this special bin is associated with a 15% bonus on the fee to be paid for the provision of the garbage collection service. In order to get the discount, users have to use this container at least 4 times a month for 10 out of 12 months of the year. In Kitakyushu, Japan, the city applies the "environmental tax" imposed on the landfill of industrial waste. Since the tax is not levied on intermediate treatments, it is also expected to promote company recycling activities and reduce any waste generated by them. Moreover, the Dutch government implements the DIFTAR system, a collecting scheme based on differentiated tariffs, which provides incentives to improve waste separation at source. This scheme enables authorities to charge for the amount of waste generated while rewarding the effort of people who minimise waste and maximise separate collection (OECD, 2020[3]).

### *Regulatory gap*

Green public procurement (GPP) in Granada, including circular economy principles, is not implemented. While the guidelines for municipal procurement of the municipality of Granada incorporate some specific environmental objectives (e.g. emission of noise, gases or other pollutants, energy consumption, disposal, decommissioning or recycling costs, etc.), there is no mandatory minimum threshold for environmental criteria in public procurement processes (Granada City Council, n.d.[10]). In 2017, the Ministry of Agriculture, Livestock, Fisheries and Sustainable Development of the Autonomous Region of Andalusia joined other eight partner countries from Europe on the project Green Public Procurement for Resource-Efficient Regional Growth – GPP4GROWTH. By 2021, the government of the Autonomous Region of Andalusia will have to prioritise GPP, increase by 7% the number of companies that integrate environmental factors and costs in the production of goods, supplies, services and works and raise awareness of the benefits of GPP in the adoption of sustainable consumption and production models (Interreg Europe, 2019[11]).

## References

Charbit, C. and M. Michalun (2009), "Mind the Gaps: Managing Mutual Dependence in Relations among Levels of Government", *OECD Working Papers on Public Governance*, No. 14, OECD Publishing, Paris, https://dx.doi.org/10.1787/221253707200. [1]

Cotec Foundation (2017), *The Circular Economy in Spain*, https://cotec.es/proyecto/informe-economia-circular-en-espana-2017/ (accessed on 29 January 2021). [6]

EC (2018), *Monitoring Framework for the Circular Economy*, European Commission, https://ec.europa.eu/environment/circular-economy/pdf/monitoring-framework.pdf (accessed on 1 February 2021). [8]

Government of Spain (2020), *España Circular 2030, Estrategia Española de Economía Circular*. [7]

Granada City Council (2020), *Callejero Fiscal por Categorías*, https://www.granada.org/inet/wcallfis.nsf/wwcall1!OpenView&Start=1&Count=30&Expand=1#1 (accessed on 7 April 2021). [9]

Granada City Council (2013), *Plan de Movilidad Urbana Sostenible de Granada*. [4]

Granada City Council (n.d.), *Instrucciones para la contratación pública sostenible, eficiente e integradora*. [10]

Interreg Europe (2019), *Project Summary - Green Public Procurement to Achieve Green Growth*, https://www.interregeurope.eu/gpp4growth/ (accessed on 11 January 2021). [11]

OECD (2020), *The Circular Economy in Cities and Regions: Synthesis Report*, OECD Urban Studies, OECD Publishing, Paris, https://dx.doi.org/10.1787/10ac6ae4-en. [3]

OECD (2011), *Water Governance in OECD Countries: A Multi-level Approach*, OECD Studies on Water, OECD Publishing, Paris, https://dx.doi.org/10.1787/9789264119284-en. [2]

Vega Sierra Elvira Consortium (2021), *Consortio*, Vega Sierra Elvira Consortium, https://www.consvega.com/consorcio/#target (accessed on 28 January 2021). [5]

# 4 Policy recommendations and actions for a circular economy in Granada, Spain

In response to the challenges identified in Chapter 3, this chapter suggests policy recommendations to implement the circular economy in the city of Granada, Spain. The city of Granada can act as: i) *promoter* of a circular economy culture and lead by example; ii) *facilitator*, for enhancing collaboration across stakeholders and levels of governments; and iii) *enabler*, for implementing the necessary regulatory and financial conditions, amongst others, in the transition from a linear to a circular economy.

## The governance of the circular economy in cities and regions

According to the OECD, cities and regions can play a role as *promoter*, *facilitator* and *enabler* of the circular economy (Figure 4.1) (OECD, 2020[1]).

- *Promoters*: Cities can promote the circular economy, acting as a role model, providing clear information and establishing goals and targets, in particular through: defining who does what and leading by example (roles and responsibilities); developing a circular economy strategy with clear goals and actions (strategic vision); promoting a circular economy culture and enhancing trust (awareness and transparency).

- *Facilitators*: Cities and regions can facilitate connections and dialogue and provide soft and hard infrastructure for new circular businesses, in particular through: implementing effective multi-level governance (co-ordination); fostering system thinking (policy coherence); facilitating collaboration amongst public, not-for-profit actors and businesses (stakeholder engagement); and adopting a functional approach (appropriate scale).

- *Enablers*: Cities and regions create the enabling conditions for the transition to a circular economy to happen, for example: identify the regulatory instruments that need to be adapted to foster the transition to the circular economy (regulation); help mobilise financial resources and allocate them efficiently (financing); adapt human and technical resources to the challenges to be met (capacity building); support business development (innovation); and generate an information system and assess results (data and assessment).

**Figure 4.1. The governance of the circular economy in cities and regions: A Checklist for Action**

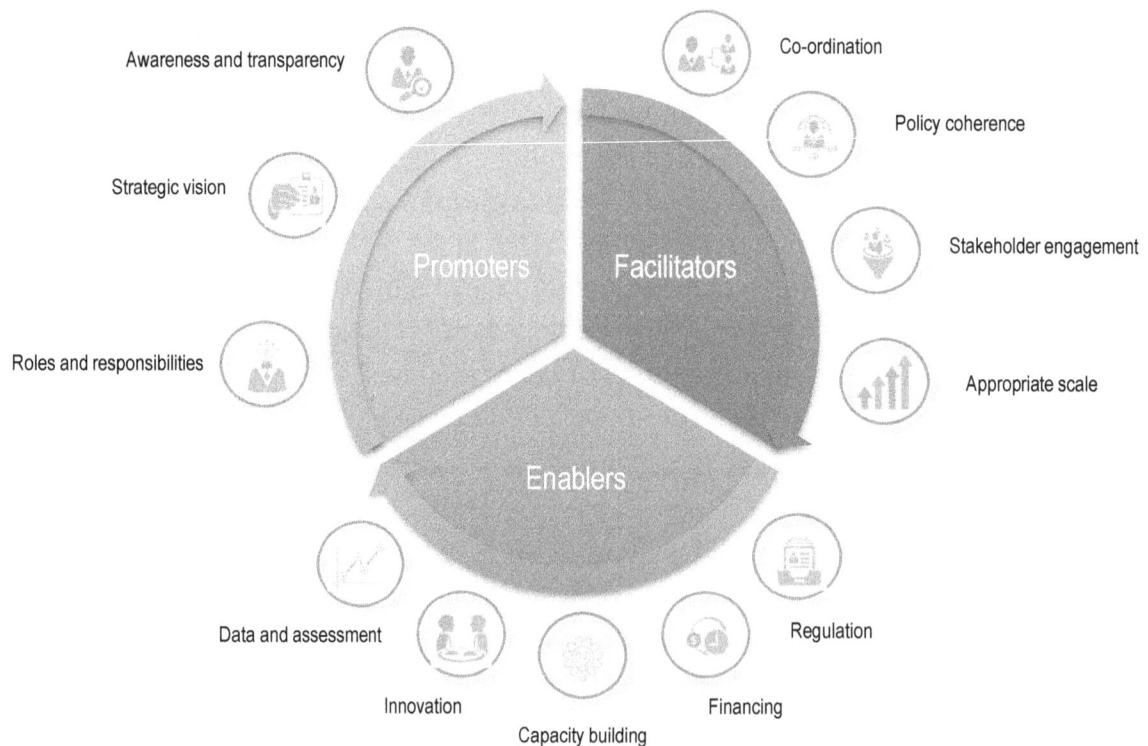

Source: OECD (2020[1]), *The Circular Economy in Cities and Regions: Synthesis Report*, https://doi.org/10.1787/10ac6ae4-en.

This chapter suggests policy recommendations and related actions based on international practices and as a result of the interviews with more than 70 stakeholders (Figure 4.2), during the OECD mission on 25-28 March 2019 and a policy seminar on 23 October 2020 (Table 4.1). The 12 governance dimensions for each cluster (promoter, facilitator and enabler) build on the Checklist for Action for cities and regions transitioning to the circular economy (OECD, 2020[1]). These governance dimensions were inspired by the OECD Principles on Water Governance (OECD, 2018[2]; 2015[3]) and they are accompanied by the OECD Scoreboard on the Governance of the Circular Economy, developed thanks to the collective efforts from case studies on the circular economy in several cities (OECD, 2020[4]; 2020[5]; 2020[6]).

It is important to note that:

- **Actions are neither compulsory nor binding**: Identified actions address a variety of ways to implement and achieve objectives. However, they are neither compulsory nor binding. They represent suggestions, for which adequacy and feasibility should be carefully evaluated by the city of Granada in an inclusive manner, involving stakeholders as appropriate. In turn, the combination of more than one action can be explored, if necessary.

- **Prioritisation of actions should be considered**: Taking into account the unfeasibility of addressing all recommendations at the same time, prioritisation is key. As such, steps taken towards a circular transition should be progressive. Table 4.1 provides an indicative timetable for actions (short, medium and long term).

- **Resources for implementation should be assessed**: The implementation of actions will require human, technical and financial resources. When prioritising and assessing the adequacy and feasibility of the suggested actions, the resources needed to put them in practice should be carefully evaluated, as well as the role of stakeholders that can contribute to the implementation phase.

- **The proposed actions should be updated in the future**: New potential steps and objectives may emerge as actions start to be implemented.

- **Several stakeholders should contribute to their implementation**: Policy recommendations and related actions should be implemented as a shared responsibility across a wide range of actors. The stakeholder groups contributing to this report and the identification of the actions are represented in Figure 4.2. They have a key role as "do-ers" of the circular economy system in Granada, Spain, along with other stakeholders that will be engaged in the future. Table 4.1 provides an indicative, however not exhaustive, selection of actors that can contribute to each of the proposed actions.

## Table 4.1. Policy recommendations and actions for the circular economy in Granada, Spain

| Role | Governance dimension | Action | Short-term | Medium-term | Long-term | Selected leading actors |
|---|---|---|---|---|---|---|
| Promoter | Roles and responsibilities | Create a dedicated municipal coordinating structure for the circular economy, building on the experience of the Municipal Office of Innovation, Smart City and Funds for Transformation. | X | | | Municipal Office of the Circular Economy<br>Municipal Department for the Environment<br>Municipal Department for Public Works and Urban Development<br>Municipal Department for Economy, Participated Companies, Treasury and Innovation<br>Municipal Office of Innovation, Smart City and Funds for Transformation |
| | | Identify who can do what within the municipal departments to apply circular economy principles in order to lead by example. Actions would include:<br>• Prevent waste generation.<br>• Promote the use of secondary materials and sustainable products.<br>• Adopt business models shifting from ownership to services.<br>• Adopt green public procurement (GPP), including circular economy principles. | | X | | Municipal Office of the Circular Economy<br>All municipal departments of the municipality of Granada |
| | Strategic vision | Collaborate with universities for urban metabolism analysis. | X | | | Municipal Office of the Circular Economy<br>University of Granada |
| | | Map the existing circular economy-related initiatives in Granada. | | X | | Municipal Office of the Circular Economy<br>Emasagra<br>Inagra<br>Municipalities within the Metropolitan Area of Granada<br>OnGranada<br>University of Granada<br>Government of Andalusia<br>Province of Andalusia<br>Granada Health Technology Park<br>Granada Convention Bureau |

| Role | Governance dimension | Action | Short-term | Medium-term | Long-term | Selected leading actors |
|---|---|---|---|---|---|---|
| | | | | | | Provincial Federation of Hospitality and Tourism Companies of Granada |
| | | | | | | Sustainable Construction Cluster of Andalusia |
| | | Link the biofactory to the urban factory. | | | X | Emasagra |
| | | | | | | Municipal Office of the Circular Economy |
| | | Define clear and achievable goals, actions and expected outcomes linked to European Union (EU) and international frameworks. | | X | | Municipal Office of the Circular Economy (in consultation with stakeholders) |
| | | Establish sector-specific goals, such as for the tourism sector. | | X | | Municipal Office of the Circular Economy |
| | | | | | | Emasagra |
| | | | | | | Inagra |
| | | | | | | Granada Convention Bureau |
| | | | | | | Provincial Federation of Hospitality and Tourism Companies of Granada |
| | | | | | | Sustainable Construction Cluster of Andalusia |
| | | Link the strategy to the local budget of the municipality of Granada. | | X | | Municipal Office of the Circular Economy |
| | | | | | | Municipal Department for Economy, Participated Companies, Treasury and Innovation |
| | | Engage stakeholders to develop a circular economy strategy. | X | | | Municipal Office of the Circular Economy |
| | | | | | | Granada Chamber of Commerce and Industry |
| | | | | | | Non-governmental organisations (NGOs) |
| | | | | | | Representatives from the private sector: |
| | | | | | | • Bioeconomy and agro-food |
| | | | | | | • Built environment |
| | | | | | | • Energy |
| | | | | | | • Retail |
| | | | | | | • Technology and science |
| | | | | | | • Tourism, restaurants, hotels and events |
| | | | | | | • Waste |
| | | | | | | • Water |
| | | Monitor regularly the progress made, evaluate the impacts and communicate the results to the public. | | | X | Municipal Office of the Circular Economy |

| Role | Governance dimension | Action | Short-term | Medium-term | Long-term | Selected leading actors |
|---|---|---|---|---|---|---|
| | Awareness and transparency | Set up an online or offline platform to gather all the existing circular economy initiatives in the city and to share information and data. | X | | | Municipal Office of the Circular Economy<br>University of Granada<br>OnGranada<br>Granada Health Technology Park |
| | | Strengthen and expand the existing awareness raising and communication initiatives. | | X | | University of Granada<br>Municipal Health, Education and Youth Department |
| Facilitator | Co-ordination | Explore options to strengthen horizontal and vertical co-ordination. | X | | | Horizontal level: Municipal departments<br>Vertical level: Provincial Council of Granada, Autonomous Region of Andalucia and the Government of Spain |
| | | Promote dialogue for co-operation on waste prevention and management; local food production and distribution, tourism and transport within the metropolitan area. | | X | | Municipal Office of the Circular Economy<br>Municipalities within the Metropolitan Area of Granada, Granada Network of Municipalities for Sustainability (GRAMAS) |
| | Policy coherence | Identify synergies across existing and future climate change, smart cities, waste management initiatives in Granada. | X | | | Municipal Office of the Circular Economy<br>All municipal departments |
| | Stakeholder engagement | Establish collaborations around the circular economy with relevant players (e.g. universities, sector-specific clusters, consumer associations and citizens). | X | | | Municipal Office of the Circular Economy<br>All municipal departments of the municipality of Granada<br>University of Granada<br>OnGranada<br>Granada Health Technology Park<br>Sustainable Construction Cluster of Andalusia<br>Representatives from the private sector:<br>• Bioeconomy and agro-food<br>• Built environment<br>• Energy<br>• Retail<br>• Technology and science<br>• Tourism, restaurants, hotels and events<br>• Waste |

| Role | Governance dimension | Action | Short-term | Medium-term | Long-term | Selected leading actors |
|---|---|---|---|---|---|---|
| | Appropriate scale | Experiment with circular economy projects at small scales (e.g. neighbourhoods). | | X | | Water  Granada Chamber of Commerce and Industry<br>Municipal Office of the Circular Economy<br>Municipal Office of Innovation, Smart City and Funds for Transformation<br>University of Granada<br>NGOs<br>Associations |
| | | Facilitate territorial linkages between the city of Granada and its surrounding rural areas. | | X | | Municipal Office of the Circular Economy<br>GRAMAS<br>Granada Agro-Food Cooperatives (FAECA) |
| Enabler | Regulation | Include circular economy principles in GPP. | | X | | Municipal Office of the Circular Economy<br>Government of Andalusia<br>Provincial Council of Granada |
| | | Apply a life-cycle analysis approach. | | X | | Municipal Office of the Circular Economy<br>University of Granada |
| | Financing | Explore funding options to accelerate the transition to the circular economy. | X | | | Municipal Office of the Circular Economy<br>Government of Andalusia<br>Provincial Council of Granada |
| | | Explore participation in European calls as a source of funding for the circular economy. | | X | | Municipal Office of the Circular Economy<br>Government of Andalusia<br>Provincial Council of Granada |
| | | Identify the economic instruments to foster the transition to the circular economy. | X | | | Municipal Office of the Circular Economy<br>Government of Andalusia<br>Provincial Council of Granada |
| | Capacity building | Review and analyse the required skills and capacities for carrying out all activities associated with designing, setting, implementing and monitoring the circular economy strategy. This could include the capacity to:<br>• Design circular economy plans/programmes that are realistic, result-oriented, tailored and coherent with national and regional objectives. | | X | | Municipal Office of the Circular Economy<br>Granada Chamber of Commerce and Industry<br>Government of Andalusia<br>Provincial Council of Granada |

| Role | Governance dimension | Action | Short-term | Medium-term | Long-term | Selected leading actors |
|---|---|---|---|---|---|---|
| | | • Involve stakeholders in the planning of the circular economy strategy.<br>• Ensure adequate financial resources by linking strategic plans to multi-annual budgets and to mobilise private sector financing.<br>• Collect and analyse data, monitor progress and carry out evaluations. | | | | |
| | | Identify existing training and educational programmes at the university level to establish possible synergies and provide support if need be. | | X | | Municipal Office of the Circular Economy |
| | | Collaborate with the University of Granada and other institutions to develop targeted capacity building programmes for public officials. | | | X | Municipal Office of the Circular Economy<br>University of Granada |
| | Innovation | Create an incubator to promote circular economy projects. | | | X | OnGranada<br>University of Granada<br>Granada Chamber of Commerce and Industry |
| | | Organise initiatives for the collaborative development of ideas for implementation in the most relevant sectors of the city (e.g. challenges). | | | X | Municipal Office of the Circular Economy<br>Municipal Office of Innovation, Smart City and Funds for Transformation<br>University of Granada<br>OnGranada<br>Granada Chamber of Commerce and Industry |
| | | Facilitate the use of quick response (QR) codes to share information across the value chains, in particular on the quality and maintenance of a product and the creation of online platforms. | | | X | Municipal Office of the Circular Economy<br>Municipal Office of Innovation, Smart City and Funds for Transformation<br>Granada Health Technology Park<br>University of Granada |
| | | Create a single window for the circular economy for businesses. | | X | | Municipal Office of the Circular Economy |
| | Data and assessment | Generate an information, monitoring and evaluation system on the circular economy. | | X | | Municipal Office of the Circular Economy<br>Municipal Office of Innovation, Smart City and Funds for Transformation |

| Role | Governance dimension | Action | Short-term | Medium-term | Long-term | Selected leading actors |
|------|---------------------|--------|------------|-------------|-----------|------------------------|
| | | | | | | University of Granada |
| | | Explore the innovative solutions that big data, the Internet of Things (IoT), machine learning and blockchain tools can provide to the circular economy (e.g. real-time information to make last-mile logistics more efficient). | | X | | Municipal Office of the Circular Economy<br>Municipal Office of Innovation, Smart City and Funds for Transformation<br>OnGranada<br>Granada Health Technology Park<br>University of Granada |

# Figure 4.2. Stakeholders map in Granada, Spain

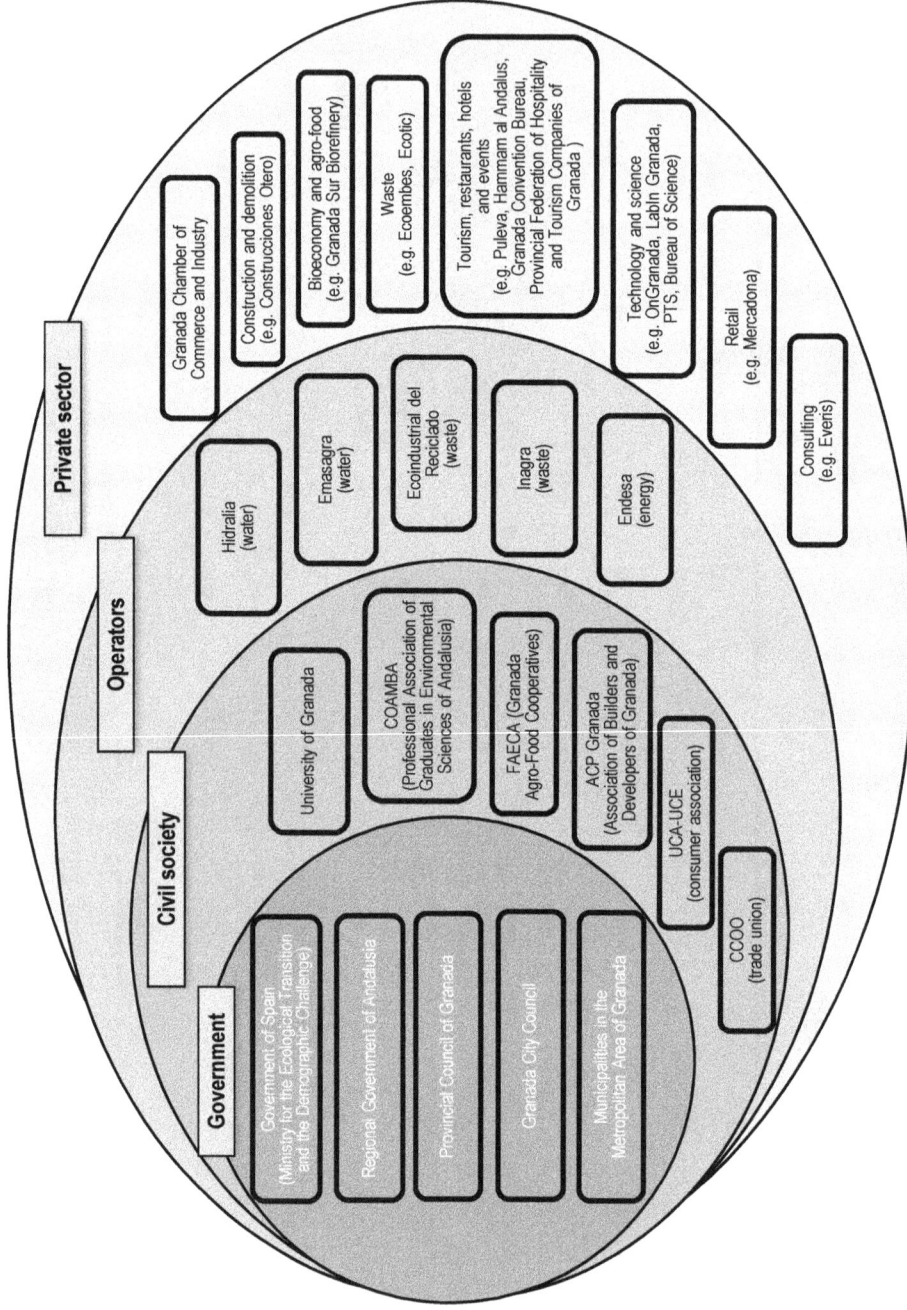

Note: This is a map based on interviews with more than 70 stakeholders that took part in the OECD mission to the city of Granada on 25-28 March 2019 and in the virtual policy seminar on 30 October 2020. The institutional mapping builds on earlier OECD Water Governance Reviews (OECD, 2015[7]; 2019[8]).

## Promoter

As promoter, the city of Granada can: i) create a dedicated municipal structure for the circular economy and lead by example; ii) develop a strategic vision on the circular economy; and iii) promote a circular economy culture.

### *Roles and responsibilities*

Creating a dedicated municipal structure for the circular economy could help co-ordinate actions towards the circular economy transition across municipal departments. The circular economy is still an incipient concept for the city of Granada but the transition from a linear to a circular economy will require leadership, collaboration across stakeholders and co-ordination across municipal departments and levels of government. The dedicated office could help embed circular economy principles into municipal policies and practices, in order to lead by example. Actions would include:

- Prevent waste generation (e.g. plans to prevent waste production; reduce the use of paper or banning single-use plastics such as cups in municipal events and daily activities).
- Promote the use of secondary materials and sustainable products and the introduction of circular economy principles in the construction of roads and buildings.
- Adopt business models shifting from ownership to services (e.g. product-as-a-service model through public procurement: pay for a lighting service adapted to the municipality's needs rather than buying light bulbs and appliances; lease a furniture service instead of buying specific furniture, etc.).
- Adopt GPP, including circular economy principles (e.g. reuse, durability, reparability, purchase of second-hand or remanufactured products).

The Circular Economy Office could identify and create synergies across urban strategies. As an example, in the last 3 years, the city has put in place several initiatives for making the city "smarter", such as the Granada Smart City 2020, launched in 2018 by the Municipal Department for Economy, Finance and Smart City. Moreover, in 2021, the city of Granada created a Municipal Office of Innovation, Smart City and Funds for Transformation to move towards building a smart city and working towards greater effectiveness and efficiency in the delivery of municipal services. The office depends on the mayor's office and is transversal across municipal departments. The political willingness, the leadership and the technical competencies led to the achievement of the following results: installation of free WiFi hotspots throughout the city, the installation of sensors to monitor air quality and noise in the city and the development of training programmes on digital skills for municipal staff. The city could build on the experience of the Office of Innovation, Smart City and Funds for Transformation and create a dedicated structure to move forward the circular economy agenda. This structure should be characterised by a cross-departmental and transversal nature. The creation of the Andalusian Circular Economy Office as the administrative body in charge of the transition, planned in the draft Circular Economy Law of Andalusia, could be an interesting example to follow. The Circular Economy Office could coordinate actions also at metropolitan level, in agreement with neighbouring municipalities.

There are many practices at the international level, which can be inspiring for Granada. Several cities (e.g. Nantes Metropolitan Area, France; Rotterdam, the Netherlands) have set up specific dedicated circular economy offices within the municipal departments, taking the lead of circular economy-related initiatives, making sure that circular economy principles are included in local policies and that the municipality itself applies circular economy principles in daily activities and operational management: from waste management to replacing ownership with services, last-mile distribution practices, etc. Other cities carry out the same functions through innovation offices (e.g. Antwerp, Belgium; Sabadell, Spain), environment agencies (e.g. Copenhagen, Denmark; Joensuu, Finland), economic development and co-operation offices (e.g. Dunedin, New Zealand; Kitakyushu, Japan), urban planning and sustainability offices (e.g. Milan, Italy; Oulu, Finland), waste management utility companies or agencies (e.g. Greater Porto Area, Portugal; Toronto, Canada), city council/municipal central administrations (e.g. Murcia, Spain; Prato, Italy) and public works (e.g. Phoenix, United States) (OECD, 2020[9]).

### Strategic vision

The city of Granada could develop a strategic vision of the circular economy to clarify objectives and identify actions to achieve them, reduce fragmentation of policies and silos, and optimise costs and synergies across stakeholders. According to the OECD (2020[1]), there are various steps for developing and implementing a circular economy strategy: i) analyse stock and flows; ii) map the existing circular economy-related initiatives; iii) define clear and achievable goals, actions and expected outcomes; iv) allocate budget and resources to each of the actions; v) share and co-create the strategy with stakeholders to build consensus; vi) monitor regularly the progress made and evaluate the impacts.

The city of Granada, through the office in charge of setting and implementing the circular economy vision in co-ordination with municipal departments, could:

- *Collaborate with the universities to analyse stock and flows*, in order to identify the city's priorities based on the analysis of consumption and production trends and material flows, as well as identify key sectors potentially able to implement circular economy principles and practices. The University of Granada could lead the urban metabolism analysis. Results of the analysis should be disseminated and clearly communicated to all relevant stakeholders in Granada (Figure 4.2). The analysis should be replicated after a certain period of time (e.g. 2-3 years) to evaluate changing production and consumption paths and modify the priorities.

- *Map the existing circular economy-related initiatives in Granada.* The mapping can be carried out through an online platform to upload initiatives and projects in the field of the circular economy, or through offline platforms, gathering input from stakeholders through regular meetings, surveys, interviews and public consultations. For example, in 2021, the city of Umeå, Sweden, collaborated with the Circular Regions initiative to develop a platform (Circular Regions Platform) to map the existing circular initiatives in the city, identifying best practices by business model, impact and cycle phases, among others (Circular Regions, 2021[10]). The Regional Government of Catalonia (Spain) created a Circular Economy Observatory (*Observatorio de Economía Circular de Cataluña*) whose main objective is to map circular initiatives in Catalonia. For the case of Granada, it would be particularly relevant to execute the mapping at the metropolitan area level for building synergies at the right scale.

- *Link the biofactory to the urban factory.* The strategy could build on positive examples for the circular economy, such as the one provided by Emasagra concerning the water sector, through the biofactory, closing loops across water, energy and waste. For example, the biofactory should connect to the urban factory for sustainable food production and use waste streams or enhance innovation with the industrial symbiosis.

- *Define clear and achievable goals, actions and expected outcomes linked to EU and international frameworks.* Objectives could be linked to the 2030 Agenda for Sustainable Development. In particular, the circular economy strictly relates to United Nations Sustainable Development Goal (SDG) 12, pledging for more sustainable and responsible consumption and production patterns. Moreover, it is also relevant for the achievement of SDGs 6 (water), 7 (energy), 11 (sustainable cities and communities), 13 (climate action) and 15 (life on land). The European Green Deal and the New Action Plan for the Circular Economy (2020), which sets the objective of achieving climate neutrality, are key frameworks to consider for developing circular economy actions.

- *Establish sector-specific goals,* in relation to economic activities, such as tourism, that have strong impacts on the city in terms of economic growth and environmental consequences of related activities (e.g. transport, waste). Identify circular chains in the "culture" and "hospitality" sectors, which are key for the local economy (Box 4.1). Some areas of action could consist in:

  o Setting up a network of circular hotels. For example, the Circular Hotels Leaders Group (*Kloplopergroep*) was recently launched in Amsterdam. A total of 12 hotels have started co-operating among them and with actors along their different value chains. These actions can lead to new circular opportunities. Exchanging knowledge, joint purchasing and bundling of waste streams or working with suppliers within each value chain are part of the actions that can be put forward (e.g. collaborating with the textile sector's suppliers to find more sustainable uses of textiles in the hospitality sector and reduce the sector's carbon footprint) (CREM, 2018[11]). The city of Granada could explore setting up a similar initiative with the Provincial Federation of Hospitality and Tourism Companies of Granada.

  o Promoting sustainable mobility and last-mile logistics as a way to reduce carbon emissions by reducing traffic and the use of raw materials. Applying reverse logistics[1] could be one way of doing this, reducing logistic costs and increasing resource efficiency by connecting local demand and supply in real-time.

  o Promoting anti-food waste campaigns and actions across restaurants and bars.

  o Rewarding circular businesses in the cultural, touristic and hospitality sectors with certificates.

---

**Box 4.1. Examples of circular economy practices in the culture sector from the city of Paris, France**

In November 2018, the city of Paris adopted its Second Roadmap of the Local Circular Economy Plan. The strategy includes 15 new specific actions, including in the culture sector. The city of Paris further developed a practical guide aiming at "developing the circular economy in Parisian cultural spaces and institutions" which included the following recommendations:

- Commit to certification and standards relating to the circular economy, by encouraging event organisers to sign up for a Parisian environmentally responsible standard.

- Adapt cultural programmes to raise awareness and engage cultural actors in the circular economy by developing cultural programmes in relation to the circular economy (conferences, collections, residencies, etc.) and create space for dialogues with artists, curators and art directors on this topic. For example, each semester, the Canopée La Fontaine's media library organises talks with academics, writers or non-profit organisations specialised in sustainable development and the circular economy.

- Adjust contracts and public procurement processes by integrating performance targets and clauses in the procurement of frequently used products, promoting renting rather than buying and including circular and environmental criteria to the various consultations and tenders.

- Develop plans and build internal capacity on the circular economy in the cultural space. For example, the French Museum of Natural History in Paris recruits trainees who specialise in sustainable development and circular economy to work on the sustainable development area of the museum.

- Add environmental criteria to the catering contracts whether for general catering in restaurants and cafés or for specific events such as opening buffets. The city of Paris has developed a guide for organising environmentally friendly events.

---

- Improve waste management by equipping sites such as recycling bins, vermicomposting or outdoor composting.

- Support the adoption of eco-design and reuse practices by donating or reselling scenography materials and elements and creating a network of local partners for the redistribution of materials and elements. Adaptive reuse of cultural heritage sites (retrofitting, rehabilitation or redevelopment) also appears as a way to promote a circular economy in cultural cities. For example, the city of Paris signed a charter to develop "pop-up art" (temporary occupation of sites) in Paris, with about 15 public and private partners and the objective to rehabilitate the existing sites, make new experiments and rethink the urban space.

Source: City of Paris, (2018[12]), *Second Roadmap of the Circular Economy Plan for Paris*, https://www.apisite.paris.fr/paris/public/2019%2F1%2FVDP_PEC_2E_FEUILLE_DE_ROUTE_WEB.pdf; City of Paris (2020[13]), *Practical Guide: Developing the Circular Economy in Parisian Cultural Spaces and Institutions*; Foster, G. (2020[14]), "Circular economy strategies for adaptive reuse of cultural heritage buildings to reduce environmental impacts", http://dx.doi.org/10.1016/j.resconrec.2019.104507.

- *Linking the strategy to the local budget of the municipality of Granada* in order to ensure adequate financial resources and ensure human resources are adequate for the implementation of the action.

- *Engaging stakeholders to develop a circular economy strategy.* The circular economy is a shared responsibility across stakeholders that need to be involved from the beginning of the process. Many international initiatives on the circular economy foresee stakeholder consultation (Box 4.2). Granada could engage stakeholders from different levels of government, civil society and the private sector. For the latter, in order to get the message across to a larger number of businesses, the municipality could collaborate with sectoral associations (e.g. ACP Granada, COAMBA, FAECA) and the Granada Chamber of Commerce and Industry to spread the message to the business sector. Building on the recommendations provided in the OECD Checklist for Stakeholder Engagement in Water Governance (OECD, 2015[15]), some steps to be followed by Granada might include:

  o Designing a participatory methodology to engage key stakeholders in the definition and co-creation of a shared circular economy strategy that reflects their concerns:

    – Map all stakeholders that have a stake in the outcome or are likely to be affected, as well as their responsibility, core motivations and interactions.

    – Define the ultimate line of decision-making, the objectives of stakeholder engagement and the expected use of input.

    – Use stakeholder engagement techniques, ensuring the effective representation of all stakeholders in the process.

    – Allocate proper financial and human resources and share needed information for result-oriented stakeholder engagement.

    – Regularly assess the process and outcomes of stakeholder engagement to learn, adjust and improve accordingly.

    – Embed engagement processes in clear legal and policy frameworks, organisational structures/principles and responsible authorities.

    – Customise the type and level of engagement to the needs and keeping the process flexible to changing circumstances.

    – Clarify how the inputs gathered from consulted stakeholders will be used.

  o Creating participation spaces for citizens and stakeholders throughout the different implementation phases of the circular economy strategy. Instruments that can be used to share the ownership of the circular economy transition with stakeholders include:

- Multi-stakeholder fora.
- Workshops.
- Breakfast meetings on the circular economy.
- Co-creation methodologies.
- Feedback loops.

---

**Box 4.2. Select international examples of stakeholder engagement in circular economy initiatives**

The role of bottom-up public consultation mechanisms is significant on the road to circularity, as a starting point to collect ideas and proposals from stakeholders. National and local governments have taken action in this regard. For example:

- In Italy, the Ministry of the Environment promoted a two-month online consultation on the national strategic document on the circular economy. About 3 900 people took part in the consultations and 300 organisations and institutions provided specific comments on the proposed text.
- A key step for the development of the Spanish Strategy on the Circular Economy was the "Pact for a circular economy", engaging the main economic and social stakeholders in Spain towards circular business models. By September 2019, a total of 347 stakeholders had adhered to the pact.
- The Circular Economy Strategy of Greater Paris, France, was developed by 240 stakeholders from over 120 different organisations. They were divided into working groups and defined 65 proposals.
- In Brussels, Belgium, consultations across stakeholder allowed the identification of priority areas for circular economy projects.

Source: OECD (2020[11]), *The Circular Economy in Cities and Regions: Synthesis Report*, https://doi.org/10.1787/10ac6ae4-en.

---

- *Regularly monitoring the progress made* (e.g. quantity of circular economy-related projects, number of circular building to be constructed, etc.), *evaluating the impacts and communicating the results to the public.* Table 4.2 suggests a number of indicators for setting and implementing a circular economy strategy (OECD, 2020[11]). Moreover, it is relevant for the city of Granada to follow up on the monitoring efforts in Andalusia, since the Andalusian Circular Bioeconomy Strategy plans to design a series of indicators. Due to the similarities in economic structures between the city of Granada and Andalusia mentioned in Chapter 1, the city of Granada could consider co-ordination with the region for measuring progress.

**Table 4.2. Selected indicators for setting and implementing a circular economy strategy**

| Phase | Type of indicator | Indicators for the circular economy strategy: Input, process and output |
|---|---|---|
| Setting the strategy | Process | No. of public administrations/departments involved |
| | Process | No. of stakeholders involved |
| | Input/process | No. of actions identified to achieve the objectives |
| | Input/process | No. of projects to implement the actions |
| | Process | No. of projects financed by the city/regional government/Total number of projects |

| Phase | Type of indicator | Indicators for the circular economy strategy: Input, process and output |
|---|---|---|
| | Process | No. of projects financed by the private sector/Total number of projects |
| | Process | No. of staff employed for the circular economy initiative and implementation within the city/region/administration |
| Implementing the strategy | Environmental output | Waste diverted from landfill (t/inhabitant/year or %) |
| | Environmental output | $CO_2$ emission saved (t $CO_2$/capita or %) |
| | Environmental output | Raw material avoided (t/inhabitant/year or %) |
| | Environmental output | Use of recovered material (t/inhabitant/year or %) |
| | Environmental output | Energy savings (Kgoe/inhabitant/year or %) |
| | Environmental output | Water savings (ML/inhabitant/year or %) |
| | Socio-economic output | No. of new circular businesses (e.g. companies, start-up, etc.) created to implement the circular economy initiative |
| | Socio-economic output | No. of businesses (e.g. companies, start-ups, etc.) adopting circular economy principles |
| | Socio-economic output | Economic benefits (e.g. through additional revenue and costs saving) (EUR/year) |
| | Socio-economic output | No. of employees of new circular businesses |
| | Socio-economic output | No. of jobs created from circular activities |
| | Governance output | No. of companies coached by the city/region to adopt circular economy principles |
| | Governance output | No. of contracts awarded by the purchasing department of the city/region that include a circular economy criterion/Total number of contracts |
| | Governance output | City/region % of public investment dedicated to the circular economy initiative/Total public investment by the city/region |

Source: OECD (2020[1]), *The Circular Economy in Cities and Regions: Synthesis Report*, https://doi.org/10.1787/10ac6ae4-en.

### Awareness and transparency

The city of Granada could promote a *circular economy culture* among citizens, businesses and relevant actors and encourage sustainable production and consumption practices. There are many ways through which to increase awareness and share information of circular economy opportunities and practices. For example, the city of Valladolid, Spain, organises Circular Weekends, during which entrepreneurs connect with one another and join forces for circular projects. In Granada, it is important to move from the notion of the circular economy as synonymous with sustainable waste management and investigate upstream options for narrowing and slowing loops, based on eco-design and reuse. The city of Granada, in collaboration with the University of Granada, could consider introducing a label for local circular activities, for instance, related to food (e.g. restaurants), construction or other sectors (examples are provided in Box 4.3).

Moreover, the existing clusters (e.g. CSA, OnGranada), technological parks (e.g. Granada Health Technology Park [PTS]), research institutions (e.g. University of Granada), associations in the city (e.g. ACP Granada, COAMBA, FAECA, UCA-UCE, etc.) could promote the circular economy based on their own specialisation, whether technology, food or hospitality. Learning by example is important for followers of the circular economy transition. For example, the city of London, United Kingdom, recruited "circular economy ambassadors" in different companies and local authorities to share the benefits of the circular economy with specific information for each economic sector and to raise awareness at the workplace (London Waste and Recycling Board, 2017[16]).

The city, in cooperation with research centres, could strengthen and expand the existing educational initiatives in schools. The Circular Economy and Recycling: The Solution for the Environment programme designed by the Health, Education and Youth Department of the municipality of Granada for students from primary school, secondary school and higher education is a good practical example of raising awareness.

The city of Granada could adapt the content of the programme according to the age group and could also explore opportunities to address other topics related to the circular economy beyond recycling.

Finally, the city of Granada could create an online platform to gather all existing circular economy initiatives in the city and share information and data relating to the circular economy. This platform should be regularly updated and easily accessible. However, it is important to note that the lack of access to high-quality access to internet could be an issue for some municipalities of the province. There are several digital tools implemented in other cities that could be inspirational. For example, the Austin Materials Marketplace and Austin Reuse Directory is an online searchable directory to inform residents of nearby outlets to reuse items, such as drop-off locations, pick-up services and resale options. The city of Phoenix, United States, developed an online Recycle Right Wizard to provide recycling information to local residents and has also launched a digital educational website, Recycle+, which promotes a digital interaction with the residents on recycling best practices through activities, games, resource guides and educational videos.

In addition, a website and information shared through social media can reach a certain type of population, such as young people, and quickly inform about initiatives, projects and how to actively participate. However, as evidenced by the trend of the ageing population in Granada, many citizens lack the knowledge to use digital applications. Therefore, it is necessary to develop adequate training programmes and ensure connectivity in order to leave no one behind in the transition to the circular economy.

---

### Box 4.3. Examples of labelled products for the circular economy

Certifications are developed to assure stakeholders and clients that products and services meet requirements linked to the circular economy. The private sector and national and subnational authorities are taking steps in this regard to develop and introduce labels for the circular economy. For example:

- The **Amsterdam Made Certificate** was developed upon request of Amsterdam City Council in the Netherlands to inform consumers about products that are made in the Amsterdam area while seeking to boost creativity, innovation, sustainability and craftsmanship.

- The French roadmap for the circular economy, **50 Measures for a 100% Circular Economy**, launched by the Ministry for an Ecological and Solidary Transition (*Ministère de la Transition Écologique et Solidaire*) in 2018, includes the deployment of voluntary environmental labelling in five pilot sectors (furnishing, textile, hotels, electronic products and food products).

- The **White Paper on the Circular Economy of Greater Paris** examines 65 proposals, including the design and use of circular economy labels. More precisely, it aims to provide higher visibility of existing environmental labels, such as the French NF Environment (a collective certification label for producers that comply with environmental quality specifications) and the European ecolabel, as well as the development of a quality label for second-hand products. The city of Paris is also making progress in the creation of the NF Habitat HQE certification, specific to the construction sector. The certification aims to define a "circular economy profile" adding new specific requirements. Besides meeting all mandatory requirements established in the NF HQE Base standards, construction projects should reach at least 40% of the criteria established in the "circular economy profile" to be considered circular (e.g. inclusion of a waste management plan, use of recycled materials, development of life analysis calculations, eco-certification of wood, considering deconstruction processes, establishing synergies with local actors in the surrounding areas, among others).

Source: French Government (2018[17]), *50 Measures for a 100% Circular Economy*, http://www.ecologique-solidaire.gouv.fr/sites/default/files/FREC%20-%20EN.pdf (accessed on 6 June 2019); Amsterdam Made (2019[18]), *Homepage*, http://www.amsterdammade.org/en/ (accessed on 6 June 2019); Paris City Council (2015[19]), *White Paper on the Circular Economy of Greater Paris*, https://api-site.paris.fr/images/77050 (accessed on 11 June 2019).

## Facilitator

As facilitator, the city of Granada can: i) facilitate co-ordination across municipal departments and across other levels of governments; ii) link the circular economy with existing initiatives; iii) engage stakeholders for the circular economy; iv) explore spatial linkages across the urban and the rural area and experiment at various scales.

### Co-ordination

At the horizontal level, co-ordination across municipal departments can help identify sector-related trade-offs and effectively implement a circular economy strategy. For example, the city of Toronto, Canada, created a Cross-Divisional Circular Economy Working Group, which is now comprised of 11 divisions to co-ordinate and increase the capacity of city divisions for implementing circular economy initiatives. The working group's mandate is to provide informed input, ideas and feedback during the development of the city's circular economy initiatives.

At the vertical level, the city of Granada, the Provincial Council of Granada, the Autonomous Region of Andalucía and the Government of Spain could benefit from mutual support to enhance synergies and achieve common goals, within the framework of a circular economy strategy. There are several initiatives that could be taken into account already and for which alignment of objectives could be taken into account. For example:

- The Andalusian Circular Bioeconomy Strategy identifies the generation of synergies and alliances between all actors in the different areas of activity of the bioeconomy, as a key factor in its implementation.
- The regional government's Strategy for Sustainable Development 2030 includes the objective of establishing inter-institutional co-ordination and co-operation mechanisms to facilitate a global framework for action.
- The Spanish National Circular Economy Strategy also highlights the importance of facilitating and promoting the creation of appropriate channels to facilitate the exchange of information and co-ordination with public administrations in order to create synergies that favour the transition.

Together with municipalities of the metropolitan area, the city of Granada could identify synergies, in order to apply circular economy principles to: reduce resource consumption and waste; preserve natural capital and ecosystem services; and design out negative externalities (economic, social and environmental) associated with resource waste, degradation of natural capital and ecosystem services. The city of Granada, the largest municipality amongst 34 municipalities[2] of the metropolitan area and the centre of the economic activities, could promote dialogue for co-operation on waste prevention and management, local food production and distribution. It could also co-ordinate activities in relation to tourists and transport to diversify the offer and reduce negative impacts due to mass tourism. Some cities have set up co-ordination mechanisms either with neighbouring municipalities or across levels of government, such as: dedicated horizontal working groups (e.g. Melbourne, Oulu and Toronto) and roundtables for the co-ordination of actions related to the circular economy in cities and metropolitan areas (e.g. Barcelona, Spain) (OECD, 2020[1]).

In addition, the city could explore opportunities for collaboration on the circular economy with the Granada Network of Municipalities for Sustainability (GRAMAS), promoted by the Environment Department of the Provincial Council of Granada and which includes 90 municipalities in the province, except the city of Granada. Its purpose is to provide the local entities of the province with a tool for co-operation and exchange, which allows the incorporation of the principles of sustainability and compliance with good environmental practices in order to achieve sustainable development in the management of the municipalities of Granada. There are six thematic groups addressing water, energy, urban planning, biodiversity and environmental engagement.

## Policy coherence

The city of Granada could identify linkages across existing and future initiatives in the city on climate change, smart cities, waste management, amongst others, and their respective targets that can be achieved through applying circular economy principles. For example, smart data can help with monitoring traffic and mobility to reduce $CO_2$ emissions. It can contribute to making waste collection more efficient by reducing the number of trips thanks to real-time data and improve waste sorting by providing feedback to users through mobile applications. Data platforms can also be of use in the built environment sector by providing information about the materials that have been used to construct buildings and that are potentially reusable in the future, at the end of life of the infrastructure.

There are several strategies, plans and actions led by the city of Granada that could be linked to the circular economy, such as:

- Granada's Smart City Strategic Plan 2020, which aims to turn Granada into one of Europe's intelligent cities through the implementation of new technologies in the management of municipal services and resources.
- The Air Quality Improvement Plan for 2017-20, which aims to improve the air quality of the city by focusing on four horizontal areas (capacity building; information; awareness-raising and collaboration; and management) and five sectors (industry; built environment; transport; agriculture and farming; and residential, commercial and institutional).
- The Green Ring Road (*Anillo verde*) project, a public-private collaboration for the cultivation of more than 200 000 trees by 2031.

A general overview of the existing plans that could be linked to the circular economy could foster coherence across all sectors and synergies across responsible departments.

## Stakeholder engagement

Since the circular economy is a shared responsibility across stakeholders, the city of Granada could establish collaboration around the circular economy with relevant players, including the following:

- The University of Granada (UGR) is leading many initiatives linked to the circular economy, particularly focusing on technologies that can boost the circular transition, plastics, the role of the circular economy within the implementation of the SDGs and an inclusive project on waste collection. Furthermore, the Department of Urban Planning and Land Management, and the Area of Architectural Composition of the UGR promote the debate on how to achieve a green future for Granada through the platform "Debates of Granada".
- Granada's technological and other sector-specific clusters support innovation and circular business. For example, the OnGranada technological cluster works on projects related to reusing waste and increasing resource efficiency. The Granada Health Technology Park (PTS) provides teaching, research and business development services to companies working in the pharmaceutical, health sciences and healthcare sectors. Furthermore, construction companies that are members of the Sustainable Construction Cluster of Andalusia (CSA) are increasingly recovering materials from construction and demolition waste.
- Several associations representing the private sector and consumers have also been carrying out actions, mainly to raise awareness of the circular economy. Some of the actions completed or planned by these groups are: creating a platform for secondary products; granting certificates for

companies to evidence a level of commitment to sustainable development; designing environmental indicators; and workshops to build knowledge on the opportunities from recycling.

Collaborations can be established through sectoral and cross-sectoral networks for the circular economy (e.g. National Platform for Circular Manufacturing initiative 2020-22, CIRCULEIRE in Ireland and Sustainable Restaurants Network in Umeå, Sweden), incubators or innovation platforms (e.g. Paris & Co in Paris, France, and the Circular Economy Hub in Groningen, the Netherlands) and networking events (e.g. Circular Glasgow in Glasgow, United Kingdom) (Box 4.4). Finally, involving citizens in the circular transition of Granada is key to achieve willingness and commitment, as they make constant consumption choices and can influence production.

---

### Box 4.4. Stakeholder engagement in cities and regions

Cities and regions apply different typologies of stakeholder engagement towards the circular transition but mainly stakeholders are engaged through consultation. The various types and levels of stakeholder engagement identified in the OECD *Stakeholder Engagement for Inclusive Water Governance* (2015[15]) are equally relevant for securing the social and political buy-in needed for the transition to a circular economy:

- *Communication*: Aims to make the targeted audience more knowledgeable and sensitive to a specific issue.
- *Consultation*: Aims at gathering stakeholders' comments, perceptions, information, advice, experiences and ideas.
- *Participation*: Allows stakeholders to take part in the decision-making process and in discussions and activities.
- *Representation*: Attempts to develop a collective choice by aggregating preferences from various stakeholders and often consists in having stakeholders' perspectives and interests officially represented in the management of a project or of an organisation.
- *Partnership*: Consists of an agreed-upon collaboration between institutions, organisations or citizen fora to combine resources and competencies in relation to a common project or challenge to solve.
- *Co-decision* and *co-production* are the ultimate levels of stakeholder engagement as they are characterised by a balanced share of power over the policy or project decision-making process.

From the 51 cities and regions surveyed in OECD (2020[1]), 27% had organised consultation activities, followed by communication (25%), participation (19%), partnership (13%), and only represent 10% for co-decision and co-production initiatives (Figure 4.3).

Figure 4.3. Type of stakeholder engagement for the circular economy in 51 surveyed cities and regions

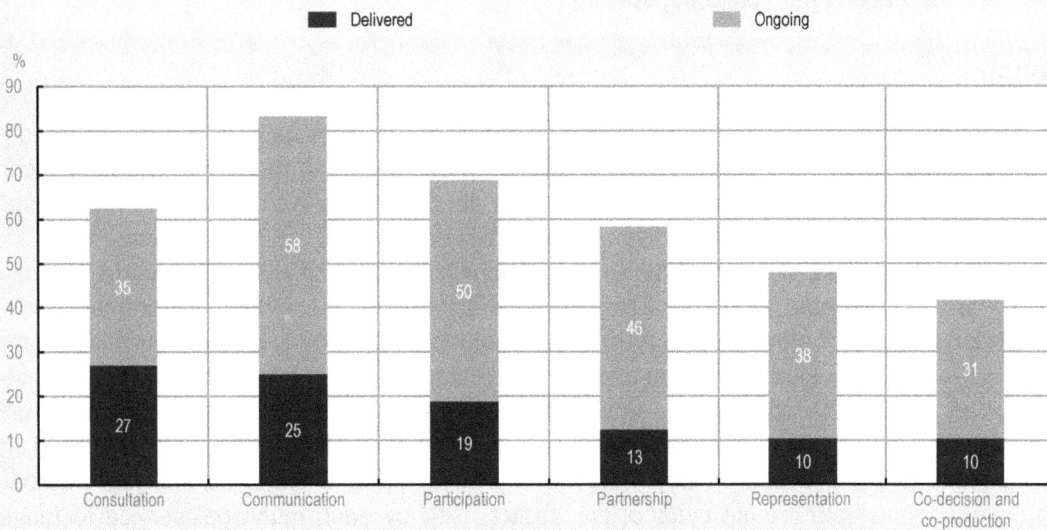

Source: OECD (2020[1]), *The Circular Economy in Cities and Regions: Synthesis Report*, https://doi.org/10.1787/10ac6ae4-en; OECD (2015[15]), *Stakeholder Engagement for Inclusive Water Governance*, https://doi.org/10.1787/9789264231122-en.

## *Appropriate scale*

The city of Granada could be a "circular lab" to experiment pilots in different neighbourhoods within the city, for example for smart waste collection. In terms of experimentation and pilots at the neighbourhood level, Valladolid, Spain, started a pilot project to meet the target of separate collection by 60% by 2030. Another example in the city of Amsterdam, the Netherlands, is the development of a circular neighbourhood, the Circular Buiksloterham. Once one of the most polluted areas in the city, it is now turning into a circular area through the development and construction of circular and sustainable buildings, receiving sustainable energy supply generated at the local level, the experimentation with smart grid solutions and the creation of parking spaces for bicycles and shared mobility options.

In the case of Granada, agriculture shows great potential for the connection of urban and rural areas within a circular economy approach. These sectors are of major relevance both in the economy and in the employment of the province of Granada, above the Spanish average. The city of Granada could explore opportunities to promote agreements with food suppliers of public canteens in the city of Granada based on nearby producers (e.g. from the Vega de Granada) or create circular loops in the agro-food and bioeconomy sector, use organic waste as fertiliser, last-mile type of food production and distribution, etc. There are several international experiences in urban-rural connections within a circular economy that could be inspirational for Granada. For example, Kitakyushu City, Japan, has established a food-recycling loop between rural-urban areas to use compost generated in urban areas as fertilisers in rural areas or as a source of energy for the city, while in Tampere, Finland, eco fellows are co-ordinating rural-urban partnerships related to biogas. They work as a hub that brings together different actors that have not been necessarily in contact before (farms, power plant operators, logistics etc.).

## Enabler

As enabler, the city of Granada can: i) implement GPP; ii) identify fiscal and economic instruments for the circular economy; iii) foster capacity building for the circular economy; iv) support business development; v) develop an information and monitoring system.

### *Regulation*

Circular economy principles could be included in GPP to promote eco-efficiency, eco-design and collaborative consumption. The guidelines for municipal procurement of the city of Granada incorporate some social and environmental policy objectives, such as: promoting the social and labour insertion of people with physical and/or intellectual disabilities; stability and quality in employment; improvement of occupational health and safety; corporate social responsibility; and criteria of fair trade, ethical public procurement and sustainable products. Environmental criteria for the award of contracts include the emission of noise, gases or other pollutants, energy consumption, disposal, decommissioning or recycling costs, etc. However, the evaluation criteria and the establishment of a minimum threshold are determined in each tender, making the value of the environmental criteria in the award of the contract unknown (Granada City Council, 2017[20]). Some international examples of cities including circular criteria into their purchasing process are available in Box 4.5. The city could apply a life-cycle analysis approach and develop criteria to evaluate the life cycle of the assets used by each municipal service to foster more sustainable solutions in municipal services.

---

**Box 4.5. Green public procurement for the circular economy: Examples from cities**

In OECD member countries, public procurement accounts for approximately 12% of gross domestic product (GDP) and subnational governments, including cities, are responsible for around 63% of public procurement. Almost all OECD countries have developed strategies or policies to support GPP. High-impact sectors are construction, food and catering, vehicles and energy-using products.

According to the European Commission, the impact of public procurement on the transition to a circular economy is worth around EUR 2 trillion in the EU, around 14% of GDP. There are several examples of GPP that includes circular criteria:

- Amsterdam, the Netherlands, has developed its *Roadmap for Circular Land Tendering* that includes 32 performance-based indicators for circular economy building developments.

- Zurich, Switzerland, took the decision to lease printing equipment rather than buying it outright, thus only paying per page printed and incentivising better printer performance and energy use.

- Bollnäs, Sweden, has applied what the local government calls "functional public procurement" (*funktionsupphandlingen*) to rent light as a service in municipal pre-schools and schools. The service is provided by a start-up that received support from Umeå's BIC Factory business incubator.

- Flanders, Belgium, implemented the Green Deal Circular Procurement (GDCP) between 2017 and 2019. Inspired by the Dutch Green Deal on Circular Purchasing (launched in 2013), the joint project was signed by 162 participants (companies and organisations), the Flemish Minister of the Environment and its initiators Circular Flanders, The Shift, the Association of Flemish Cities and Municipalities (VVSG) and the Federation for a Better Environment (BBL). In total, 108 purchasing organisations, local authorities, companies, financial institutions and 54 facilitators have been involved. During the 2 years of the initiative, the signatories of the GDCP have conducted more than 100 circular procurement pilot experimentations, building

---

knowledge and experience and testing tools and methodologies and new forms of chain co-operation.

- Ljubljana, Slovenia, included environmental requirements in its tenders as part of the technical specifications, as a condition for determining the qualifications of the provider or as a criterion for selecting the most favourable bid.

Some of the obstacles identified in pursuing GPP include: the perception that green products and services may be more expensive than conventional ones; public officials' lack of technical knowledge on integrating environmental standards in the procurement process; and the absence of monitoring mechanisms to evaluate the achievements of goals.

Source: OECD (2015[21]), *OECD Recommendation of the Council on Public Procurement*, http://www.oecd.org/gov/ethics/OECDRecommendation-on-Public-Procurement.pdf (accessed on 6 June 2019); Municipality of Amsterdam (2017[22]), *Roadmap Circular Land Tendering*, https://amsterdamsmartcity.com/projects/roadmap-circular-land-tendering (accessed on 28 January 2020); EC (2017[23]), *Public Procurement for a Circular Economy: Good Practice and Guidance*, https://ec.europa.eu/environment/gpp/pdf/Public_procurement_circular_economy_brochure.pdf (accessed on 7 November 2019); Municipality of Bollnäs (2018[24]), "New light with many advantages", https://www.bollnas.se/index.php/88-aktuellt/2525-nytt-ljus-med-manga-foerdelar (accessed on 28 January 2020); The Shift (2019[25]), *Green Deal Circular Procurement in Flanders*, https://theshift.be/en/projects/greendeal-circular-procurement-in-flanders (accessed on 28 January 2020); OVAM (2020[26]), *Green Deal Circular Purchasing*, http://www.vlaanderen-circulair.be/nl/onze-projecten/detail/green-deal-circulair-aankopen (accessed on 5 February 2020); OECD (2020[1]), *The Circular Economy in Cities and Regions: Synthesis Report*, https://doi.org/10.1787/10ac6ae4-en.

### Financing

The city of Granada could explore funding options to accelerate the transition to the circular economy, supporting businesses and community-based initiatives. For example, the city of Amsterdam, the Netherlands, through the Amsterdam Climate and Energy Fund (ACEF) and the Sustainability Fund invested in more than 65 projects related to climate, sustainability and air quality for a total of EUR 30 million. These are revolving funds, allowing to reinvest revenues within 15 years to fund additional sustainable energy production, energy efficiency or circular economy projects. Each of the funded projects must contribute to the aims of the sustainability agenda approved by the city council in 2015. Regarding the nature of the financing, the ACEF provides funding in the form of loans, warranties and/or share capital, subject to a maximum of EUR 5 million per project. The London Waste and Recycling Board (LWARB) supports circular business through the Circular Economy Business Support Programme. The venture capital fund supports circular economy small- and medium-sized enterprises (SMEs) in scaling up businesses that are already in the market. Moreover, the LWARB, through the Circularity European Growth Fund operated by Circularity Capital, seeks investment opportunities in circular businesses with proven cash flow and profit.

There are also European calls that could be explored as a source of funding for the circular economy, such as:

- Horizon Europe: The new 2021-27 EU funding programme for research and innovation has a budget of EUR 95.5 billion and includes an area of intervention on circular systems (EC, 2021[27]).
- Invest EU Programme: Focusing on investment, innovation and job creation in Europe over the period 2021-27, its scope is to support a sustainable recovery for a greener, more digital and more resilient European economy (EU, 2021[28]).
- The new LIFE programme: It is expected to include calls for project proposals on the circular economy (EC, 2021[29]).

The city of Granada could identify the economic instruments to foster the transition to the circular economy. Co-ordination with the national and regional government may be required. A range of economic instruments are used in cities to incentivise or disincentive individual behaviours, such as:

- Property tax according to the energy consumption of buildings.
- Corporate income tax (e.g. based on the waste generation level, water and energy consumption, use of recycled materials as raw materials).
- Value added tax (VAT) reduction on products labelled as circular (e.g. easy to recycle and reuse, proximity).
- Tax reductions on second-hand materials.
- Discount waste fees according to preselected criteria.
- Differentiated tariffs for waste separation and recycling (e.g. pay-as-you-throw approach).

Some international experiences include the following: the Dutch Government's DIFTAR system is a scheme based on differentiated tariffs in order to provide incentives to improve waste separation at source (pay-as-you-throw); VAT reductions for companies working on circular economy projects in Shanghai, China, and for reused items in Sweden; discounts on waste fees for businesses in Milan, Italy, and San Francisco, United States.

### *Capacity building*

The city of Granada could foster capacity building for the circular economy to provide municipal staff with deeper knowledge and is taking its first steps in the transition towards the circular economy. Due to the incipient state of the circular transition in the city, it is necessary to develop capacities both in the municipality and the business environment. As such, the city can:

- Review and analyse the required skills and capacities for carrying out all the activities associated with designing, setting, implementing and monitoring the circular economy strategy. This could include the capacity to:
  - Design circular economy plans/programmes that are realistic, result-oriented, tailored and coherent with national and regional objectives.
  - Involve stakeholders in the planning of the circular economy strategy.
  - Ensure adequate financial resources by linking strategic plans to multi-annual budgets and mobilising private sector financing.
  - Collect and analyse data, monitor progress and carry out evaluations.
- Identify existing training and educational programmes at the university level to establish possible synergies and provide support if need be.
- Collaborate with the University of Granada and other institutions to develop targeted capacity building programmes for public officials.

Specific skills are needed for future circular economy jobs. The Amsterdam Metropolitan Area (AMA), the Netherlands, identified six groups of skills relevant to future circular jobs: basic skills (capacities that facilitate acquiring new knowledge); complex problem solving (abilities to solve new, complex problems in real-world settings); resource management skills (capacities for efficient resource allocation); social skills (abilities to work with people towards achieving common goals); system skills (capacities to understand, evaluate and enhance "sociotechnical systems"); and technical skills (competencies to design, arrange, use and repair machines and technological systems) (Circle Economy, 2020[30]).

### Innovation

The city of Granada could create an incubator to promote circular economy projects. An incubator should support innovative projects related to the circular economy by: providing management and business assistance; promoting connections with strategic partners in the private, public and academic sectors; facilitating access to financial opportunities (investors, loans, public programmes); and providing a physical space for the projects to develop. For example, since 2016, the Prodock, the scale-up incubator of the port of Amsterdam, the Netherlands, has been helping growing business and established companies to co-create solutions in a shared working space on diverse topics that go from transforming wet waste into renewable gas to the production of sustainable bio-based chemicals, or recycling plastic and soap waste in the hospitality sector. It is important to create conditions in which universities and companies can connect and solve the needs of the municipality. At the same time, the municipality can be a launching customer for new projects and innovations that, if successful, can be scaled up.

The city could also organise initiatives for the collaborative development of ideas for implementation in the most relevant sectors of the city (e.g. hospitality and tourism). These initiatives could take the form of "challenges" involving academia, business and government. Some international examples could be inspirational for the implementation of this initiative. For instance, in Amsterdam, the Netherlands, the Startup in Residence programme connects start-ups and scale-ups with key social challenges in the city. The municipality shares problems with a start-up that will try to develop specific solutions that can be purchased by the city.

The city of Granada, in collaboration with technological centres, could facilitate the use of QR codes to share information across the value chains. For example, codes can be used for the quality and maintenance of a product. Moreover, the data obtained through the QR codes could be useful to run predictive models to facilitate decision-making processes (e.g. estimating the economic, social and environmental impacts of the introduction of a tax).

Finally, the city of Granada could also create a single window for the circular economy for businesses, in order to offer services, information and administrative support related to circular economy projects in the city. Having a single focal point could also be beneficial for the engagement of entrepreneurs and SMEs through the reduction of transaction costs. For example, the initiative Start-up Slovenia, established in 2014, mobilises a network of mentors from various backgrounds to provide entrepreneurs and young firms with tailored advice.

### Data and assessment

Generating information and a monitoring and evaluation system would help the city of Granada reach a better understanding of what the circular economy is and improve policymaking and implementation. A wide range of data can support the monitoring and evaluation of policies, programmes and strategies, and improve policymaking and implementation, such as:

- Environmental data (e.g. resources, waste and circulation processes), flows (water, energy, products, food, transportation, information, people) and social data (circular jobs created).
- Data on empty buildings, materials used for construction and waste streams.

- Data on existing circular economy initiatives, as well as laws and regulations that can foster the transition from the linear to the circular economy.

- Data collected within the Granada's Smart City Strategic Plan 2020 taking place in the city by exploring opportunities to enable circular economy-related activities. Data collected by this initiative include real-time traffic and air quality, among others.

The city of Granada could explore the innovative solutions that big data, the IoT, machine learning and blockchain tools can provide to the circular economy (e.g. real-time information to make last-mile logistics more efficient) in Granada (Box 4.6). Digitalisation plays an important role in this case, as big data, the IoT and blockchain tools can provide real-time information, enable material traceability and foster reuse through online platforms and applications. By using available digital tools, the city of Granada can generate open data sources, make collected data publicly accessible, understandable and updated regularly. For example, the Circular City Data programme is a project promoting a collaboration between start-ups, city agencies and larger firms to collect, produce, access and exchange circular data aiming to build new and sustainable social, economic and environmental models in New York City, United States (New Lab City, 2019[31]).

Finally, the city of Granada could carry out a self-assessment of the current situation of the circular economy in Granada through the OECD Scoreboard on the Governance of the Circular Economy. This scoreboard is intended as a self-assessment tool based on the 12 key governance dimensions that would enable a circular economy system to take place (Box 4.7).

---

### Box 4.6. Blockchain solutions for the circular economy

A blockchain is a distributed append-only database, which is capable of storing any type of data and is replicated across many locations operated jointly by all users. Once added to the blockchain, a record is encrypted and cannot be changed or deleted without the knowledge of all participants. This immutability feature of blockchains is what makes them strong and an alternative to traditional centralised databases.

For the circular economy transition, blockchain technologies offer several opportunities, such as to:

- Enhance information flows along the value chain

- Improve the transparency and traceability for producers, consumers and recyclers.

- Drive the uptake of new business models, for instance through monetising plastic waste or marketing collected plastic to recycling firms with transparent information about its origin.

Using blockchain solutions still require significant amounts of energy to make its environmental footprint significant. Moreover, some questions remain about data privacy, liability and competition.

Source: IFC (2017[32]), "Beyond fintech: Leveraging blockchain for more sustainable and inclusive supply chains", https://www.ifc.org/wps/wcm/connect/85fb81a9-632c-4c98-86fc-2a0619996562/; OECD (2019[33]), *Digitalisation and the Circular Economy*, OECD, Paris.

---

### Box 4.7. The OECD Scoreboard on the Governance of the Circular Economy in cities and regions

The OECD Scoreboard on the Governance of the Circular Economy is a self-assessment tool of governance conditions to evaluate the level of advancement towards a circular economy in cities and regions. Its purpose is to accompany cities and regions in identifying gaps and assessing progress to

---

improve policies and self-assess the existence and level of implementation of enabling conditions. It is composed of 12 key dimensions, whose implementation governments and stakeholders can evaluate based on a scoreboard system, indicating the level of implementation of each dimension: Newcomer (Planned; In development), In progress (In place, not implemented; In place, partly implemented) and Advanced (In place, functioning; In place, objectives achieved). These dimensions include: 1) Roles and responsibilities; 2) Strategic vision; 3) Awareness and Transparency; 4) Co-ordination; 5) Policy coherence; 6) Stakeholder engagement; 7) Appropriate scale; 8) Regulation; 9) Financing; 10) Capacity building; 11) Innovation; 12) Data and assessment. The visualisations of the results (Figure 4.4) provide an overview of the level of circularity of a city or region for each of the 12 circular economy governance dimensions.

## Figure 4.4. Visualisation of the OECD scoreboard results

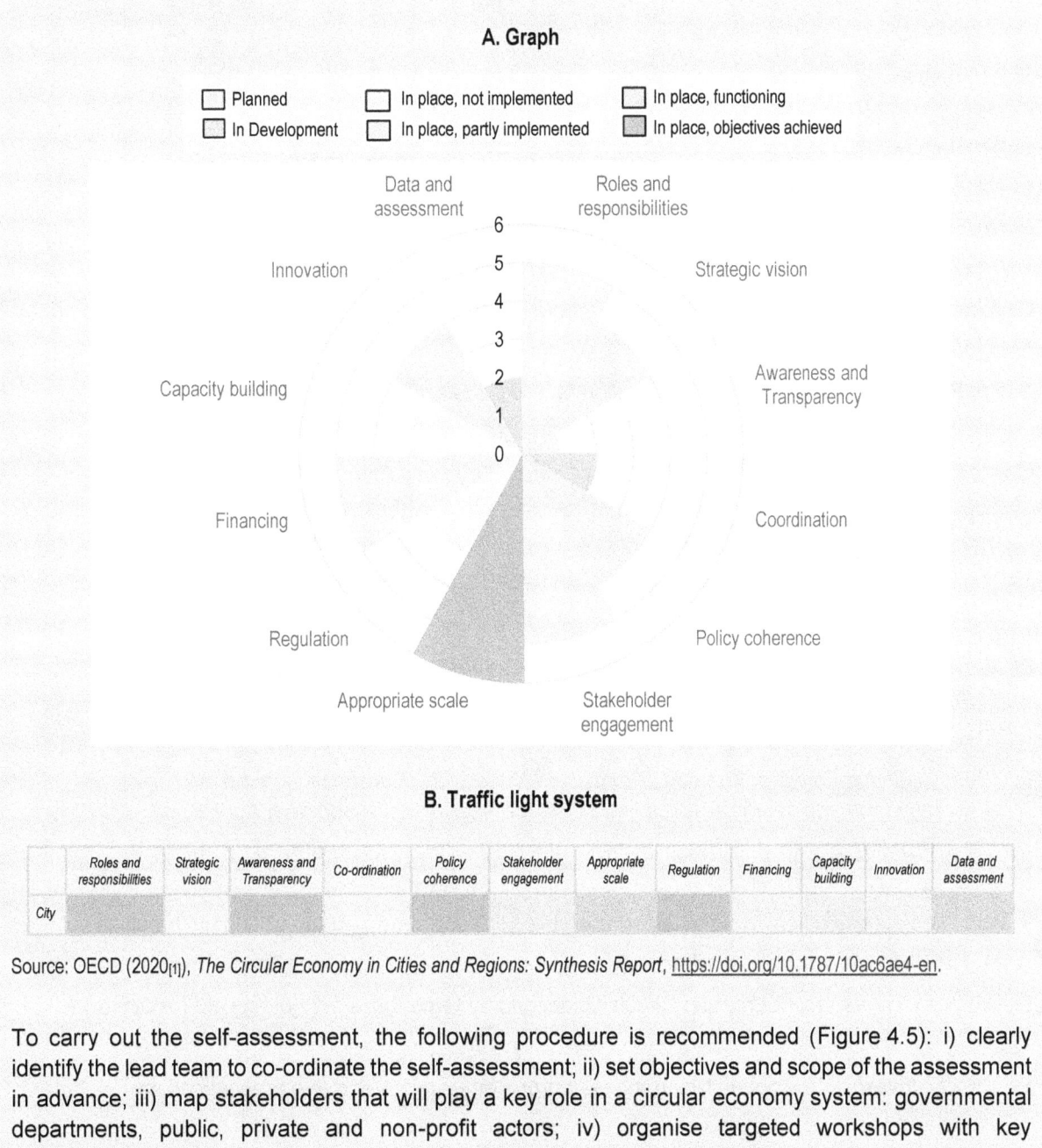

### A. Graph

Planned
In Development
In place, not implemented
In place, partly implemented
In place, functioning
In place, objectives achieved

Data and assessment · Roles and responsibilities · Innovation · Strategic vision · Capacity building · Awareness and Transparency · Financing · Coordination · Regulation · Policy coherence · Appropriate scale · Stakeholder engagement

6
5
4
3
2
1
0

### B. Traffic light system

| | Roles and responsibilities | Strategic vision | Awareness and Transparency | Co-ordination | Policy coherence | Stakeholder engagement | Appropriate scale | Regulation | Financing | Capacity building | Innovation | Data and assessment |
|---|---|---|---|---|---|---|---|---|---|---|---|---|
| City | | | | | | | | | | | | |

Source: OECD (2020[1]), *The Circular Economy in Cities and Regions: Synthesis Report*, https://doi.org/10.1787/10ac6ae4-en.

To carry out the self-assessment, the following procedure is recommended (Figure 4.5): i) clearly identify the lead team to co-ordinate the self-assessment; ii) set objectives and scope of the assessment in advance; iii) map stakeholders that will play a key role in a circular economy system: governmental departments, public, private and non-profit actors; iv) organise targeted workshops with key stakeholders to share, compare and confront views and achieve consensus; and v) repeat the process once a year to verify changes and improvements and to keep stakeholders engaged.

**Figure 4.5. A five-step self-assessment methodology**

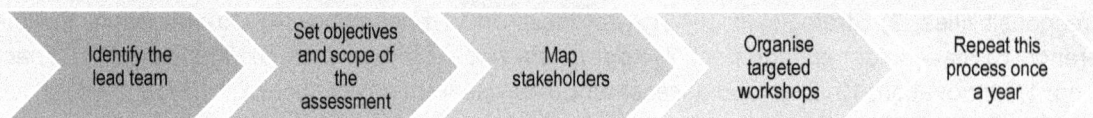

Identify the lead team ▸ Set objectives and scope of the assessment ▸ Map stakeholders ▸ Organise targeted workshops ▸ Repeat this process once a year

Source: OECD (2020[1]), *The Circular Economy in Cities and Regions: Synthesis Report*, https://doi.org/10.1787/10ac6ae4-en.

## References

Amsterdam Made (2019), *Homepage*, http://www.amsterdammade.org/en/ (accessed on 6 June 2019).                                                                                          [18]

Circle Economy (2020), *Jobs & Skills in the Circular Economy: State of Play and Future Pathways*.                                                                                       [30]

Circular Regions (2021), *Circular Regions Platform*, https://circularregions.org/ (accessed on 8 April 2021).                                                                            [10]

City of Paris (2020), *Practical Guide: Developing the Circular Economy in Parisian Cultural Spaces and Institutions*.                                                                    [13]

City of Paris (2018), *Second Roadmap of the Circular Economy Plan for Paris*, https://www.api-site.paris.fr/paris/public/2019%2F1%2FVDP_PEC_2E_FEUILLE_DE_ROUTE_WEB.pdf (accessed on 7 November 2019).                                                                      [12]

CREM (2018), *Getting Started with the Circular Hotels Leaders Group*, https://crem.nl/en/965/ (accessed on 3 February 2021).                                                             [11]

EC (2021), *Cluster 6: Food, Bioeconomy, Natural Resources, Agriculture and Environment*, European Commission, https://ec.europa.eu/info/horizon-europe/cluster-6-food-bioeconomy-natural-resources-agriculture-and-environment_en (accessed on 8 April 2021).                       [27]

EC (2021), *Moving Forward: The LIFE Programme from 2021*, European Commission, https://ec.europa.eu/easme/en/section/life/calls-proposals (accessed on 8 April 2021).               [29]

EC (2017), *Public Procurement for a Circular Economy. Good Practice and Guidance*, European Commission, https://ec.europa.eu/environment/gpp/pdf/Public_procurement_circular_economy_brochure.pdf (accessed on 7 November 2019).                                                        [23]

ECBF (n.d.), *Homepage*, European Circular Bioeconomy Fund, https://www.ecbf.vc/ (accessed on 8 April 2021).                                                                              [34]

EU (2021), *InvestEU*, European Union, https://europa.eu/investeu/home_en (accessed on 8 April 2021).                                                                                     [28]

Foster, G. (2020), "Circular economy strategies for adaptive reuse of cultural heritage buildings to reduce environmental impacts", *Resources, Conservation and Recycling*, Vol. 152, p. 104507, http://dx.doi.org/10.1016/j.resconrec.2019.104507. [14]

French Government (2018), *50 Measures for a 100% Circular Economy*, http://www.ecologique-solidaire.gouv.fr/sites/default/files/FREC%20-%20EN.pdf (accessed on 6 June 2019). [17]

Granada City Council (2017), *Instructions for Sustainable, Efficient and Inclusive Public Procurement of Granada City Council*, https://web.granada.org/inet/wordenanz.nsf/2201f0d7346e1930c12573550023beb5/e88f077bee8ce8e0c12580c2003c4cdd?OpenDocument (accessed on 6 April 2021). [20]

IFC (2017), "Beyond fintech: Leveraging blockchain for more sustainable and inclusive supply chains", https://www.ifc.org/wps/wcm/connect/85fb81a9-632c-4c98-86fc-2a0619996562/EM+Compass+Note+45+final.pdf?MOD=AJPERES&CVID=lXyrVyb (accessed on 7 April 2021). [32]

London Waste and Recycling Board (2017), *London's Circular Economy Route Map*. [16]

Municipality of Amsterdam (2017), *Roadmap Circular Land Tendering*, https://amsterdamsmartcity.com/projects/roadmap-circular-land-tendering (accessed on 28 January 2020). [22]

Municipality of Bollnäs (2018), "New light with many advantages", https://www.bollnas.se/index.php/88-aktuellt/2525-nytt-ljus-med-manga-foerdelar (accessed on 28 January 2020). [24]

New Lab City (2019), *The Circular City Research Programme. Vol I*, https://e025fd80-ac50-4e14-b81f-a09b2649b87f.filesusr.com/ugd/c3ad88_696d642dd4cc436dad96afe0369a1877.pdf (accessed on 5 May 2021). [31]

OECD (2020), *The Circular Economy in Cities and Regions*, OECD, http://dx.doi.org/10.1787/10ac6ae4-en. [9]

OECD (2020), *The Circular Economy in Cities and Regions: Synthesis Report*, OECD Urban Studies, OECD Publishing, Paris, https://dx.doi.org/10.1787/10ac6ae4-en. [1]

OECD (2020), *The Circular Economy in Groningen, the Netherlands*, OECD Urban Studies, OECD Publishing, Paris, https://dx.doi.org/10.1787/e53348d4-en. [5]

OECD (2020), *The Circular Economy in Umeå, Sweden*, OECD Urban Studies, OECD Publishing, Paris, https://dx.doi.org/10.1787/4ec5dbcd-en. [4]

OECD (2020), *The Circular Economy in Valladolid, Spain*, OECD Urban Studies, OECD Publishing, Paris, https://dx.doi.org/10.1787/95b1d56e-en. [6]

OECD (2019), *Digitalisation and the Circular Economy*, OECD, Paris. [33]

OECD (2019), *Water Governance in Argentina*, OECD Studies on Water, OECD Publishing, Paris, https://dx.doi.org/10.1787/bc9ccbf6-en. [8]

OECD (2018), *Implementing the OECD Principles on Water Governance: Indicator Framework and Evolving Practices*, OECD Studies on Water, OECD Publishing, Paris, https://dx.doi.org/10.1787/9789264292659-en. [2]

OECD (2015), *OECD Principles on Water Governance*, OECD, Paris, http://www.oecd.org/cfe/regional-policy/OECD-Principles-on-Water-Governance.pdf (accessed on 3 May 2019).   [3]

OECD (2015), *OECD Recommendation of the Council on Public Procurement*, OECD, Paris, http://www.oecd.org/gov/ethics/OECD-Recommendation-on-Public-Procurement.pdf (accessed on 6 June 2019).   [21]

OECD (2015), *Stakeholder Engagement for Inclusive Water Governance*, OECD Studies on Water, OECD Publishing, Paris, https://dx.doi.org/10.1787/9789264231122-en.   [15]

OECD (2015), *Water Resources Governance in Brazil*, OECD Studies on Water, OECD Publishing, Paris, https://dx.doi.org/10.1787/9789264238121-en.   [7]

OVAM (2020), *Green Deal Circular Purchasing*, Vlaanderen Circulair, http://www.vlaanderen-circulair.be/nl/onze-projecten/detail/green-deal-circulair-aankopen (accessed on 5 February 2020).   [26]

Paris City Council (2015), *White Paper on the Circular Economy of Greater Paris*, https://api-site.paris.fr/images/77050 (accessed on 11 June 2019).   [19]

The Shift (2019), *Green Deal Circular Procurement in Flanders*, https://theshift.be/en/projects/green-deal-circular-procurement-in-flanders (accessed on 28 January 2020).   [25]

## Notes

[1] This is the process of planning, implementing, and controlling the efficient, cost effective flow of raw materials, in-process inventory, finished goods and related information from the point of origin to the point of consumption for the purpose of conforming to customer requirements.

[2] Albolote, Alfacar, Alhendín, Armilla, Atarfe, Cájar, Cenes de la Vega, Chauchina, Churriana de la Vega, Cijuela, Colomera, Cúllar Vega, Dílar, Fuente Vaqueros, Gójar, Granada, Güevéjar, Huétor Vega, Jun, La Zubia, Láchar, Las Gabias, Maracena, Monachil, Ogíjares, Peligros, Pinos Genil, Pinos Puente, Pulianas, Santa Fe, Valderrubio, Vegas del Genil, Villa de Otura and Víznar.

# Annex A. List of stakeholders consulted during the policy dialogue

| Institution | Name |
| --- | --- |
| Acento Comunicación | Gustavo Gómez |
| ACP Granada (Association of Builders and Developers of Granada) | Francisco Martinez-Cañavate |
| ACSA Obras e Infraestructuras | Manuel Castillero |
| ACSA Obras e Infraestructuras | Antonio Fernandez |
| Bioloxa Gestión Energética | Jose Bonifacio Cuevas |
| Biomasa del Guadalquivir | Rafael García |
| CCOO (Workers Commissions) | Daniel Mesa |
| COAMBA (Professional Association of Environmental Science Graduates of Andalusia) | Andrés Ferrer |
| COAMBA (Professional Association of Environmental Science Graduates of Andalusia) | José Alfonso Gálvez |
| Construcciones Otero | Isabel Nieto |
| Covirán | Sheila Villalobos |
| Dhul | Javier Sánchez |
| Ecoindustria del Reciclado | Antonio Davó |
| Ecoindustria del Reciclado | Ignacio Figueruela |
| Ecoindustria del Reciclado | Emilio Gómez |
| Emasagra | Alejandro Muñoz |
| Emasagra | Mercedes Sánchez |
| Endesa | Jose Juan Bocarando |
| Endesa | Jose Pardos-Gotor |
| Endesa | Nerea De La Corte |
| Everis | Ángel Luis Teso |
| FAECA (Granada Agro-Food Cooperatives) | Esther Álvarez |
| Granada Chamber of Commerce | Isabel Contreras |
| Granada Chamber of Commerce | Azahara Molinero |
| Granada City Council | Ramón Alcaráz |
| Granada City Council | Mª Ángeles Garzó |
| Granada City Council | Pedro Guira |
| Granada City Council | Enrique Hernánde |
| Granada City Council | Juan José Ibáñez |
| Granada City Council | Roberto López |
| Granada City Council | Jorge Moreno |
| Granada City Council | Francisco Muñóz |
| Granada Convention Bureau | Eva Garde |
| Grupo De4 | Manuel García |
| Hammam al Andalus | Raúl Lozano |
| Hammam al Andalus | Ismael Tamayo |
| Hidralia | Gustavo Calero |
| Hidralia | María Cruz López Villalba |
| Inagra | Sebastian Fernández |
| Inagra | Ivan Carlos Salas |
| Inagra | Fabio Sánchez |

| Institution | Name |
|---|---|
| Irrigation Community of the Acequia Real or Gorda del Geni | Gerardo Aranda |
| Irrigation Community of the Acequia Real or Gorda del Geni | José Carlos Romera |
| onGranada | Francisco Luis Benítez |
| onGranada | Vito Episcopo |
| Plastic Sense Foundation | José Raya Aguilera |
| Provincial Council of Granada | Fernando Alguacil |
| Provincial Council of Granada | María Isabel Aznarte |
| Provincial Council of Granada | David Caldera |
| Provincial Council of Granada | Gonzalo Esteban |
| Provincial Council of Granada | Francisco Javier García |
| Provincial Council of Granada | Jorge López |
| Provincial Council of Granada | Trinidad Manrique De Lara |
| Provincial Council of Granada | Francisco Montoya |
| Provincial Council of Granada | Manuel Jesús Pérez |
| Provincial Council of Granada | Lucas Ruiz |
| Provincial Federation of Hotel Management and Tourism Companies of Granada | Antonio García |
| PTS (Granada Health Technology Park) | Juan Pablo Caballero |
| Puleva | Leopoldo Cabrera |
| Reacción Económica | Belén Suárez |
| Government of Andalusia | Alejandro Girela |
| Government of Andalusia | Enrique Mártinez |
| Government of Andalusia | Jesús Picazo |
| SEFIDE (Electronic financial services) | Jose Manuel Navarro |
| Self-employed | Jose Garcia |
| Self-employed | Diego Gil |
| Transportes Rober, S.A. | Francisco Gamez |
| UCA-UCE Consumers' Union of Andalusia | Inmaculada Rodríguez |
| UCA-UCE Consumers' Union of Andalusia | Juan Moreno Rodríguez |
| University of Granada | Jesús Banqueri |
| University of Granada | María Martín |
| University of Granada | Valentín Molina |
| University of Granada | Laura Plaza |
| University of Granada | Juan Carlos Reina |
| University of Granada | Laura Sánchez |
| University of Granada | Montserrat Zamorano |
| Vega Educa | Juan Raya Ruiz |